TRAVELLER'S GUIDE
TO THE ANCIENT WORLD

GREECE

IN THE YEAR 415 BCE

A DAVID & CHARLES BOOK

David & Charles is an F+W Publications Inc. company
4700 East Galbraith Road
Cincinnati, OH 45236
First published in the UK in 2008
Copyright © 2008 by Quid Publishing

Conceived, designed and produced by Quid Publishing
Level 4 Sheridan House, 114 Western Road,
Hove, BN3 1DD, UK
www.quidpublishing.com
Illustrations: Matt Pagett
Interior design: Lindsey Johns

A catalogue record for this book is available from the
British Library.

ISBN-13: 978-0-7153-2919-1 hardback
ISBN-10: 0-7153-2919-7 hardback

Printed in China by Midas Printing for David & Charles
Brunel House   Newton Abbot   Devon

Visit our website at www.davidandcharles.co.uk

David & Charles books are available from all good
bookshops; alternatively you can contact our Orderline
on 0870 9908222 or write to us at FREEPOST EX2
110, D&C Direct, Newton Abbot, TQ12 4ZZ (no stamp
required UK only).

TRAVELLER'S GUIDE
TO THE ANCIENT WORLD

GREECE

IN THE YEAR 415 BCE

Eric Chaline

D&C
David and Charles

CONTENTS

CONTENTS

3
SURROUNDING AREAS

5
PRACTICAL CONSIDERATIONS

4
ENTERTAINMENT ON A BUDGET

6
REFERENCES AND RESOURCES

INTRODUCTION: WHEN THIS BOOK WAS WRITTEN

THIS BOOK IS WRITTEN TO OFFER ADVICE FOR TRAVELLERS TO ATHENS, THE HOME OF DEMOCRACY, IN THE YEAR 415 BCE. TO PLACE THIS IN CONTEXT THE FOLLOWING IS A TIMELINE OF GREEK HISTORY, WITH DATES EXPRESSED AS THE NUMBER OF YEARS BEFORE THE DATE OF WRITING.

THREE SUPERPOWERS

The *oikoumene* (the known world) is divided into three spheres of influence, with the Greeks at the centre flanked by the two mighty barbarian empires of Carthage and Persia. Travelling east from mainland Greece, the Hellenic domain takes in the coasts of Thrace and the Black Sea, the cities of Asian Ionia, Crete and the Aegean islands; travelling west, the Greeks have settled the coasts of southern Gaul and northwestern Iberia, and Magna Graecia (Greater Greece), consisting of southern Italy and the greater part of Sicily.

The southern and western Mediterranean is the domain of the powerful trading empire of the Carthaginians, whose forefathers came from the city of Tyre in Phoenicia some four centuries ago. With its heartland and capital of Carthage on the North African coast, it takes in the coast of southern Iberia, the Balearic Islands, Corsica and Sardinia, and also the northeastern part of Sicily.

To the east of the Greek dominions lies the empire of the great king of Persia, Darios Nathos, who rules the greatest empire known to man, taking in all the lands from the Levant to the Indus, Anatolia, Egypt, Cyprus and Macedonia.

ATHENS AND HER EMPIRE

The term 'Athenian Empire' is actually a misnomer. In no way could it be compared in territorial extent, resources or population to the mighty Persian Empire that stretches from the Mediterranean Sea to India.

The empire of Athens consists of little actual territory that is held directly by the city itself, other than its surrounding region of Attica. The origin of this so-called empire was in an alliance of free city-states and islands that formed to fight the Persians. Hence, the 'empire' is actually a network of trading routes and tributary arrangements that is in constant flux.

The bulk of the Greek mainland is divided between several alliances of city-states, the most powerful of which is the Peloponnesian League headed by Athens' greatest rival, Sparta. Another alliance to be reckoned with is that of the Greeks of Magna Graecia (Sicily and Southern Italy). This is led by the Sicilian city of Syracuse, whose wealth and power has eclipsed that of the cities of old Greece.

THE GREEKS: A HISTORICAL TIMELINE

1200–700 years ago	Mycenaean civilisation
700–400 years ago	The Greek 'Dark Ages'
674–653 years ago	Reign of Kodros, last king of Athens
268 years ago	Archonship becomes annual
206 years ago	Archonship and laws of Drako
179 years ago	Archonship and constitution of Solon
150 years ago	First Parthenon on the Acropolis
146–95 years ago	Tyrannies of Peisistratos and Hippias
93 years ago	Reforms of Kleisthenes
84–33 years ago	Persian Wars
75 years ago	Battle of Marathon
65 years ago	Destruction of Athens by the Persians
65 years ago	Battle of Salamis
64 years ago	Battle of Plataia
63–62 years ago	Foundation of the Delian League
47–66 years ago	Democratic reforms of Ephialtes
46–14 years ago	Ascendancy of Perikles
39 years ago	Transfer of Delian treasury to Athens
33 years ago	Peace of Callias with Persia
32 years ago	Periklean building programme begins
16 years ago	Peloponnesian War begins
14 years ago	Plague in Athens and death of Perikles
6 years ago	Peace of Nikias with Sparta
Present day	Departure of Sicilian expedition

INTRODUCTION: THE MEDITERRANEAN WORLD

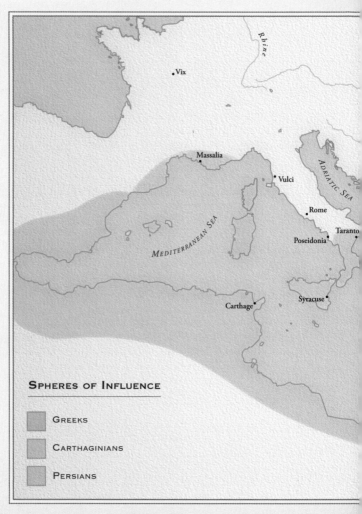

Rhine

• Vix

Massalia
•

• Vulci

ADRIATIC SEA

• Rome

MEDITERRANEAN SEA

Taranto •

Poseidonia •

Syracuse •

Carthage •

SPHERES OF INFLUENCE

GREEKS

CARTHAGINIANS

PERSIANS

A MAP OF THE MEDITERRANEAN WORLD SHOWING THE THREE MAIN SPHERES OF INFLUENCE: THE GREEKS, THE CARTHAGINIANS AND THE PERSIANS.

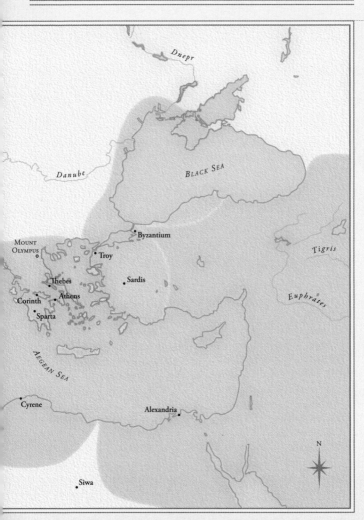

INTRODUCTION: MAKING THE MOST OF YOUR TRIP

THERE IS MUCH TO RECOMMEND A TRIP TO ATTICA AND TO ATHENS IN PARTICULAR. THE SOIL MAY BE THIN AND POOR, BUT THE REGION'S HISTORY AND CULTURE ARE RICH. THE ATHENIANS' MARITIME OUTLOOK, BACKED BY THE WEALTH UNEARTHED IN THE SILVER MINES OF LAUREION, HAS TRANSFORMED ATHENS INTO THE PRE-EMINENT CULTURAL DESTINATION OF THE EASTERN MEDITERRANEAN. AS SUCH THE CITY OFFERS THE VISITOR A WEALTH OF ATTRACTIONS, FROM ARCHITECTURE TO FESTIVALS, AND FROM HISTORY TO GREAT SPORTING CONTESTS — ATHENS HAS IT ALL.

It may take a visitor some time to travel to Athens, for while Attica's mountain ranges protect the region from invasion, they also make overland communications slow and difficult. Furthermore, Attica is bounded to the north and west by two enemies, Theban Boeotia and Peloponnesian Corinth, so it pays to travel carefully overland, and to keep the purpose of your visit to yourself.

Those travelling by sea will find that Attica is bounded by the Saronic Gulf to the south and west; while the Aegean island of Euboea shelters the eastern coast.

Attica is a land of mountains and deep valleys, with few plains. The plains of Marathon to the northeast and of Eleusis to the west of Athens have some of the most fertile land, but they are also marshy and thus prone to malaria.

CLIMATE

Attica has four distinct seasons, with cool rather than cold winters, very hot summers, and a temperate spring and autumn. Travelling during the winter is difficult, with storms at sea and flash-floods on land making either route perilous. At the height of the summer, visitors may be troubled by the oppressive heat, which afflicts the country with droughts and forest fires.

What's On When?

Visitors flock to Athens throughout the year, but especially during the spring for the City Dionysia (see p. 107); in midsummer for the great festival of Athena, the Panathenaia (see pp. 102–5); and in the autumn for the Greater Mysteries of Eleusis (see pp. 26–7). But Athens is a city of festivals, and those wishing for a quiet visit will be hard pressed to find a month in the year when she is not honouring one of her gods or heroes.

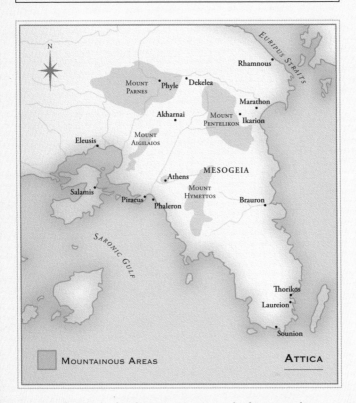

Travelling overland in the mountainous peninsula of Attica is arduous; however, Athens' excellent maritime links and harbours mean that arriving by boat is a viable option for many visitors.

A CONCISE
BACKGROUND

*Athens is one of the most ancient cities
in Greece. Among its early kings were Theseus,
who unified Attica and slew the Cretan Minotaur,
and Menestheus, who fought alongside Agamemnon
and Odysseus at Troy. But the city beloved of
Athena, goddess of wisdom and industry, was not
destined to be ruled by kings. It was the first nation in
the world to overthrow the arbitrary power of kings,
tyrants and nobles to establish the democratic
form of government now widespread in Greece.
Athens today is a thriving polis – a self-governing
city-state – of citizen smallholders, merchants
and artisans, whose freedom is guaranteed by
her 'wooden walls' – her navy.*

HISTORY: FROM FOUNDATION TO DESTRUCTION

IT IS THE PROUD BOAST OF THE ATHENIANS THAT THEY ARE DESCENDED FROM THE FOUR IONIAN TRIBES, THE ORIGINAL INHABITANTS OF GREECE, WHO, WITH THE ACHAEANS, WERE THE FOUNDERS OF MYCENAEAN CIVILISATION.

When the 350 years of the Greek 'Dark Ages' blotted out many great cities, Athens survived to emerge as one of the leading city-states of Greece. For the next three centuries Athens evolved its own unique form of government, replacing the rule of hereditary kings and *archons* with that of an assembly of free citizens. But just as 'democracy' was being born, Athens and Greece faced a great threat from the east.

The unification of Attica took place under the rule of Theseus, who is also remembered for having slain the Minotaur in the Labyrinth of Knossos.

FROM MYTH TO HISTORY

Nine centuries separate present-day Athens from the *synoikismos*, the unification of Attica into one realm, by King Theseus. To this day, remains of his palace can be seen on the Acropolis. A century and a half later, in the reign of King Kodros, the might of Mycenaean civilisation came to an end with the invasion of the Dorians.

Although many great cities of Mycenaean Greece disappeared, Athens endured, though in much-reduced circumstances. Very little is known of the city during the three centuries of the Dark Ages, but when Athens re-emerged four hundred years ago, she stood once again in the first rank of the cities of Greece.

REFORM AND REVOLUTION

After King Kodros, Athens was ruled not by kings but by life archons from among the nobility. The life term was later replaced by the decennial (ten-year) archonship, itself to be superseded by an annual

THE GREEKS

The Greeks, or Hellenes – the descendants of Hellen the man, not Helen the beauty of the Trojan War – are made up of four peoples: the Achaeans, Ionians, Aeolians and Dorians, who to this day can be identified by their different dialects, religious cults and political and cultural traditions. According to Homer, the original inhabitants of Greece were the Achaeans and the Ionians, who fought side by side in the Trojan War. The Dorians and Aeolians, the descendants of Hellen's sons Dorus and Aeolus, migrated into Greece from the north, triggering the downfall of Mycenaean civilisation and initiating the period known as the 'Dark Ages'. While some Ionians fled across the sea to settle the Aegean islands and found the cities of Asian Ionia, others took refuge behind the mountains of Attica. The proud boast of the Athenians, therefore, is that they are descendants of the first inhabitants of Greece.

archonship, whose holder was known as the 'eponymous archon', because he gave his name to the year of his reign.

Two eponymous archons, the severe Drako some two centuries ago, and the reforming Solon 27 years later, created the first written Athenian constitution and established the basis for later democratic reforms. However, 33 years after Solon's rule, the tyrant Peisistratos seized power from the nobility and ruled with the support of the common people.

Peisistratos and his sons ruled for almost 50 years, until Kleisthenes overthrew the tyranny just under a hundred years ago. He reorganised Athenian society and established democratic government and the modern legal system.

ATHENS DESTROYED

No sooner had democracy been established than there arose a threat to Athenian and Greek independence. Some 85 years ago the cities of Asian Ionia revolted against their overlord, Darios the Great of Persia. They appealed to Athens and Sparta, whose intervention led to the first Persian invasion of Greece.

A small Athenian force defeated a superior Persian army at the battle of Marathon; but a decade later Darios' son Xerxes led a huge army and fleet to Greece to avenge his father's defeat. Outnumbered, the Athenians had no choice but to abandon their city, leaving it to be destroyed by the Persians. For a time, Athens seemed to be finished.

HISTORY: RECONSTRUCTION AND EMPIRE

ALTHOUGH THE ATHENIANS WERE EVENTUALLY TRIUMPHANT, DEFEATING THE PERSIANS ON LAND AND AT SEA, ATHENS ITSELF LAY IN RUINS. DESPITE THE WAR, AND LARGELY THANKS TO PERIKLES, ATHENS HAS SINCE BEEN REBUILT AND NOW STANDS REBORN, ORNAMENTED WITH THE WORLD'S GREATEST TEMPLE, THE PARTHENON.

With the invading Persian army occupying Greece, Athens itself in ruins, and the Greek army and navy vastly outnumbered, all seemed lost. King Xerxes sat on a throne overlooking the straits between Salamis and the mainland, where the Persian navy of between 650 and 800 ships faced a Greek fleet of half that size. What followed was the greatest naval engagement of all time (see p. 95), and an overwhelming victory for the Greeks.

Disgusted, Xerxes returned to Asia, leaving an army under Mardonios to carry on the war. A year after the battle of Salamis, a Greek force of 110,000 faced a Persian army said to be three times its number at Plataia. As at Salamis, superior tactics and arms overcame sheer numbers, and the entire Persian force was annihilated.

Henceforth, Athens and its allies went on the offensive, freeing the cities of Asian Ionia and attacking Persian Egypt and Cyprus, finally forcing the Persians to sue for peace.

ATHENS TRIUMPHANT

Victory for Athens meant victory for her democracy and naval policy; however, her dealings with her Greek allies were about to change for the worse.

Sparta, a former ally, had always been wary of Athens' power, and mutual distrust finally erupted into full-scale war just 16 years ago.

While the Spartans are masters of the land and ravage Attica's fields and olive groves every year, Athens stands behind her walls, and uses her fleet to resupply her embattled cities and attack her enemies.

A peace was signed six years ago, but was soon broken, and at the time of writing Athens is planning an expedition against Syracuse in Sicily to capture grain supplies and prevent Sparta's ally sending her military assistance.

FOR THE PROTECTION OF THE STATE

Kleisthenes, the great reformer of the Athenian constitution, established the practice known as ostracism, the exile for ten years of any citizen whose banishment the Ekklesia deems necessary for the wellbeing of the state.

Once the Ekklesia has voted to hold an ostracism, it takes place two months later in the Agora, where male citizens inscribe the name of the man they want banished on *ostraka* – pieces of broken pottery. These are counted, if the total number exceeds 6,000, and the man receiving the most votes is banished for ten years.

To date, only 13 men have been ostracised. These include Xanthippus, father of Perikles; Themistokles (pictured); and Kimon – all leading citizens of Athens, whose influence was held to be dangerous, or whose political enemies saw ostracism as a means of ridding themselves of a rival.

MACHINERY OF STATE

The 500-strong Council, or *Boule*, consists of groups of 50 men chosen from each of the ten Attic tribes (see p. 23). They are selected by lot to hold office for one year, and a man can only be a councillor twice in his lifetime. The Boule's main duties are to prepare the order of business for the Ekklesia and oversee the work of civil and military officials. Each group of 50 takes turns to hold office for 36 days, during which they have to call a minimum of four assemblies. The 50 members of the standing committee of the Boule that convenes and presides over the Ekklesia are known as *prytaneis*, or senators.

The Boule meets in the Bouleuterion, and the prytaneis in the Tholos (also known as the Prytaneikon), both on the Agora. The Ekklesia usually meets every nine days, although emergency meetings are also called in time of need. Any citizen may speak in the Ekklesia, where votes are taken by a simple show of hands.

POLITICS: THE RULE OF LAW

JUST AS THE PEOPLE OF ATHENS HAVE OVERTHROWN THE ARBITRARY RULE OF KINGS, NOBLES AND PRIESTS TO MAKE THE LAWS OF THE LAND, SO THEY HAVE TAKEN INTO THEIR OWN HANDS THE POWERS TO ENFORCE THEM. THE ATHENIANS EMPLOY SEVERAL FORMS OF LEGAL JUDGEMENT, DEPENDING UPON THE NATURE AND GRAVITY OF THE CASE AT HAND. THE SIMPLEST AND MOST COMMON IS PRIVATE OR PUBLIC ARBITRATION, BUT FOR MORE SERIOUS CASES, THEY HAVE RECOURSE TO THE COURT OF THE AREOPAGOS OR TO THE JURY COURTS. THE COURTS ALSO PLAY A VITAL PART IN THE DEMOCRATIC PROCESS, FOR THEIR JURIES CAN TRY OFFICIALS FOR MISCONDUCT AND STRIKE DOWN LAWS.

For most disputes, Athenians prefer arbitration (private or public) to the jury courts. In the case of private arbitration, the parties agree to be bound by the decision of a third party, without any right of appeal unless bias can be proven on the part of the arbitrator. The alternative is to apply to the Board of Public Arbitrators to appoint an arbitrator, who can be any male citizen aged 60 or over. In this case, the arbitrator's decision can be appealed in the jury courts.

THE COURT OF THE HILL OF ARES

The court of the Areopagos was once the Senate of Athens, staffed by former archons who were chosen from among the nobility. In successive reforms, the powers of the Areopagos were gradually reduced and transferred to the Boule and Ekklesia. Ephialtes further reduced the jurisdiction of the Areopagos, so that today it has few other duties than the prosecution of murderers. However, because the Areopagites are appointed for life from among men who have served Athens as archons, their decisions are held in the utmost respect.

An Athenian trial lasts one day at most, and takes place in the Agora in front of a crowd of jurors.

A DAY IN COURT

The popular or jury courts take place in the Agora. The juries are picked every morning from a pool of 6,000 citizen volunteers, who receive a small payment for their duty – although less than a day's wage, so as to discourage sloth.

Juries are large and made up of odd numbers, ranging from 201 to 5,001. This ensures the presence of a representative cross-section of the community, avoids the possibility of a tied jury, and also reduces the effectiveness of bribery. The juror has little direction from the magistrates; he is responsible to his own conscience for his decisions and cannot be censured or punished for them.

Once the jury has been selected and sworn in, the magistrates open the proceedings. There are no advocates, and the plaintiff and defendant each pleads his case in front of the jury. Regardless of the nature, complexity or gravity of the case, all trials are limited to one day. If the defendant is found guilty, he may be subject to a predetermined penalty. Otherwise, the jury is asked to decide his sentence. In this case, the plaintiff proposes one penalty to the jury, and the defendant makes a counter-proposal. The lightest penalties are fines and loss of political rights, and the most severe are enslavement, exile and execution.

CHECKS AND BALANCES

The jury courts also have a role to play in the democratic government of Athens through their power of judicial review. If a politician should be accused of passing or even proposing a law that violates the Athenian constitution, he can be prosecuted in the courts. If he is found guilty, his law is immediately declared unconstitutional and is repealed. This, like the practice of ostracism, is another safeguard against the power of the demagogue skilled at manipulating the Ekklesia with his oratory.

PEOPLE: THE ATHENIANS

THE POPULATION OF ATTICA CONSISTS OF THREE GROUPS, DEFINED BY THEIR ORIGINS AND CIVIL RIGHTS. THE FIRST ARE FREEBORN CITIZENS OF ATHENS, BOTH NOBLE AND COMMON; THE SECOND ARE METICS, FREEBORN FOREIGNERS WHO HAVE SETTLED IN ATTICA; THE THIRD ARE SLAVES, WHO FOR THE MOST PART ARE FOREIGNERS — CAPTIVES TAKEN IN WAR OR PURCHASED FROM SLAVE TRADERS.

Some 36 years ago Perikles altered the qualifications for Athenian citizenship, restricting it to those born of two Athenian parents. His motives for doing so are unclear, but he might have done it to limit the size of the Ekklesia, or to further reduce the power of the nobility, many of whom had foreign wives. The law, however, rebounded on him, because when his son by his Athenian wife died, his only surviving heir was by his foreign mistress, Aspasia of Miletus. His popularity, however, ensured that the Ekklesia granted his son citizenship.

A CITIZEN'S DUTIES

Athenian men, both nobles and commoners, become citizens upon reaching the age of 18; however, because they have to do two years' *ephebia* (military service) they do not enter into their full civic rights until the age of 20. Thenceforth

---

WHAT TO EXPECT

POPULATION ESTIMATES FOR ATTICA

Freeborn Athenians:	130,000
Resident freeborn aliens (metics):	70,000
Slaves:	300,000
Total:	500,000

Figures include men, women and children

TRIBES, DEMES AND THIRDS

Kleisthenes reorganised the population into ten *phylai*, or tribes, each named after an Athenian hero. The tribes are further subdivided into *demoi*, or demes, of which there are 139 corresponding to urban districts, towns and villages. The demes are grouped into 30 *trittyes*, or thirds. The thirds contain demes from city, country and coastal districts, ensuring that no gulf develops between the urban and rural populations. Belonging to a tribe and deme is a prerequisite of citizenship, and a citizen is known by three names: his given name, his father's name, and his deme name: for example, Perikles, son of Xanthippus, of the deme Kolargos.

they have the duty to attend the Ekklesia, and from their 30th year they can be chosen by lot to be councillors in the Boule, jurors, magistrates or officials.

The courts can strip a criminal of his citizenship rights, and the Ekklesia can grant a foreigner citizenship for meritorious service to the city.

THE 'OTHERS'

Non-citizens fall into two distinct groups: freeborn metics, or resident aliens; and slaves.

Metics have far fewer rights than citizens. They are not allowed to take part in the civic life of the city, and they have limited property rights. They are, however, expected to fight for Athens in her army and navy. Other resident aliens of high status are wealthy merchants and the artists and intellectuals who come to build and decorate Athens' fine buildings and teach in her schools.

Slaves are for the most part captives taken in war or purchased from slave traders. They have no civic rights and are the chattels of their masters. As a rule, however, the lot of the Athenian slave is tolerable. Slaves are expected to carry out all the heavy labour in the fields, docks and factories, and the domestic work at home, but when compared to the lot of other slaves around the known world they can be considered relatively well treated. The exceptions are the slaves who work in the silver mines of Laureion (see p. 88) and those who are employed in the corn mills. There are two slave markets in Attica: at Sounion and in the Agora at Athens, held on every new moon. Depending on age, sex and skills, a slave will fetch between 200 and 600 drachmas.

RELIGION: THE OLYMPIAN GODS

THE GREEKS WORSHIP MANY GODS, GODDESSES AND DEMIGODS. BUT FIRST AMONG THEM ARE THE TWELVE IMMORTAL OLYMPIANS, HEADED BY THE KING OF THE GODS, ZEUS, MASTER OF SKY AND THUNDER. HE AND HIS SIBLINGS AND CHILDREN RULE THE DIFFERENT DOMAINS OF THE WORLD. MOST CHERISHED AMONG HIS CHILDREN IS THE GODDESS ATHENA, WHO GAVE HER NAME TO THE CITY AND GUARDS IT FROM HER SANCTUARIES ATOP THE ACROPOLIS. IN ADDITION TO THE OLYMPIANS, THE GREEKS HONOUR OTHER GODS, SUCH AS DIONYSOS, AS WELL AS SEMI-DIVINE HEROES INCLUDING HERAKLES.

THE OLYMPIAN DODEKATHEON

Zeus, king of the gods
Hera, wife of Zeus
Poseidon, god of the oceans
Demeter, goddess of fertility
Hestia, goddess of hearth
   and home
Aphrodite, goddess of beauty
   and love
Apollo, god of prophecy
   and music
Ares, god of war
Artemis, goddess of the hunt
   and childbirth
Athena, goddess of wisdom,
   craft and warriors
Hephaistos, god of smiths
Hermes, messenger of
   the gods

DIVINE FAMILY

Although they are immortal beings and live far above the human world on the summit of Mount Olympus in northern Greece, the *Dodekatheon*, or twelve Olympian gods, exhibit many human virtues and frailties. Just like their human worshippers, they are part of an extended family, with its loves, marriages, births, infidelities and feuds.

The elder Olympians themselves did not have happy family antecedents: Zeus and his siblings Hades, god of the underworld, Poseidon, Hera, Demeter and Hestia fought and defeated their own father, the titan Kronos, for mastery over the universe. Once he was defeated, Kronos was banished to the underworld.

ATHENA, PATRON OF THE CITY

Legend has it that Zeus once complained of an agonising headache. It was so bad that he asked Hephaistos to strike his head with his hammer. When Zeus' skull split open, Athena emerged full-grown and armed. She vied with Poseidon to become the protector of the city to which she gave her name, and where she is now worshipped in a number of guises.

Her most ancient and revered form is as Athena Polias (of the city), whose wooden cult image is enshrined in the Erechtheion and is carried in procession in Athens' Great Panathenaia. Her main cult image, made of ivory and gold by Pheidias, is housed in the Parthenon, which is dedicated to her aspect as Parthenos, the maiden.

Another important shrine on the Acropolis honours her as Ergane, the goddess of weaving and craft. She is also Promachos, the goddess of war and strategy; Hygieia, goddess of health and cleanliness; and Nike, goddess of victory, soon to be worshipped in a temple now being built on the bastion of the Acropolis close by the Propylaia.

CHILDREN OF ZEUS

The remaining seven Olympians are the children of Zeus by his jealous spouse Hera or his many mistresses. Ares and Hephaistos are the sons of Hera, while Aphrodite, the twins Apollo and Artemis, and Hermes are Zeus' children by different lovers. Athena (see box) is said to have been born of Zeus alone. Several other gods and goddesses are recognised by the Athenians, including Hebe, goddess of youth; Helios, the sun; Dionysios, the god of wine, who is honoured in the City and Rural Dionysia; Asklepios, god of healing; Nemesis, goddess of vengeance; Kore (Persephone), whose story is the basis for the mysteries of Eleusis (see p. 27), and the hero Heracles, famous for his 'twelve labours'.

In addition, the Athenians also have shrines to the Muses, who personify the arts, and the terrifying Erinyes, the Furies, who punish murderers and evildoers.

RELIGION: SERVING THE GODS

TO EACH OF THE GODS ARE AWARDED THE HONOURS THAT HIS OR HER POSITION DEMANDS. FIRST AMONG THE GODS OF ATHENS ARE FATHER ZEUS AND HIS FAVOURITE DAUGHTER ATHENA. THOUGH ZEUS' TEMPLE REMAINS UNFINISHED, ATHENA IS HONOURED WITH THE CITY'S MOST SPLENDID TEMPLES ON THE ACROPOLIS AND THE GREATEST OF ITS FESTIVALS. IN GREECE, WORSHIP OF THE GODS IS SO MUCH PART OF PUBLIC AND PRIVATE LIFE THAT THERE IS NO SEPARATE WORD MEANING 'RELIGION'. THE THREE MAIN OBSERVANCES ARE PRAYER, SACRIFICE AND PURIFICATION.

As you can see from wandering around the city streets, Athens abounds in splendid temples and ancient shrines dedicated to the gods. The principal shrines are to be found on the Acropolis, but temples and sanctuaries also feature in every quarter of the city, in the main public meeting place and market, the Agora, and in all the demes of Attica.

Unlike the great temples of Egypt, however, in which many secret rites and mysteries are performed, the temples of Athens are merely the storehouses for the sacred images of the gods and of the votive offerings made to them by devotees. Religious rituals are practised either on altars in front of the temples during the course of the great festivals of the city, or in private at home.

One cult is an exception to this rule, that of the Mysteries of Eleusis (see box), whose rites are performed inside the Telesterion in the presence of initiates alone.

An important part of many religious rituals in Athens is the sacrifice of animals.

WHAT TO EXPECT

THE RITES OF SPRING

The story of Kore's abduction and return is at the very heart of the mystery cult of Eleusis. Kore is the daughter of Demeter and Zeus. The younger gods all courted her, but her mother rejected them and hid her away far from Olympus.

Nevertheless, Hades, the lord of the underworld, abducted Kore and took her for his bride. Distraught, Demeter turned from a goddess of life and fertility to one of barrenness and death. Rather than see the earth die,

Zeus ordered Hermes to fetch Kore back from Hades. Kore was reunited with her mother, thereby allowing the earth to blossom once more.

During Kore's stay in the underworld, Hades tricked her into eating six pomegranate seeds, so she must return for six months of every year. Thus the seasons came into being: life flourishes in spring and summer when Kore and Demeter are reunited, and the earth becomes barren when they are parted.

TO PLEASE THE GODS

The principal rites of Greek religion are prayer, sacrifice, and purification. In sacrifice, an offering is made to the gods. This could be a libation of wine, oil, or milk, an offering of cakes, vegetables, or first fruits, or a large-scale animal sacrifice – a *hekatombe*.

All manner of animals are sacrificed to the gods, from humble chickens to bulls and horses, which are led by the priests to the altars during the great feast days of the Athenian year. Once the animal has been killed, a part of the flesh is burned for the god and the rest is butchered, cooked, and eaten as a form of sacrament between the divinity and the worshippers. Offerings of food and drink are also made to the ancestors who live on in the underworld.

Purification is needed by those who have been defiled by contact with death. A man or woman who is ritually impure cannot approach the gods and is in danger of suffering their wrath, so they are cleansed of defilement with seawater or the blood of sacrificial victims.

Domestic Life:
Hearth and Home

FOR ALL ITS FINE PUBLIC BUILDINGS AND TEMPLES, ATTICA IS NOT KNOWN FOR THE SIZE OR COMFORT OF ITS PRIVATE HOMES. IN THE POPULAR DEMES THE HOUSES ARE SMALL, OF FLIMSY CONSTRUCTION, AND WITH FEW CREATURE COMFORTS. EVEN IN THE RICHER DEMES THERE ARE FEW HOUSES OF NOTE. THE HOMES OF THE RICH ARE LARGER, OF COURSE, BUT DO NOT COMPARE TO THE MANSIONS OF PERSIA OR EGYPT IN THEIR FITTINGS AND DECORATION.

The housing stock of Athens is estimated to be around 10,000 private dwellings. In the popular demes houses rarely exceed three or four rooms, built on one floor; when they have a second storey, this is accessible by an external staircase. The walls are of mud, wood or loosely mortared brick or stone, and are so poorly built that burglary is rife. The miscreant's favoured method for gaining entry is to dig through the walls; hence burglars are known here as 'wall-piercers'.

The poorer houses have no kitchens, bathrooms or latrines. Windows are small to keep out the winter cold and summer heat, and smoke from cooking is allowed to escape through a hole in the roof, opened by the expedient of moving a roof tile when needed. Care should be taken when walking through the narrow streets of the city, not just because of the emptying of chamber pots, but also because front doors open outwards and can catch the unwary pedestrian a sudden blow.

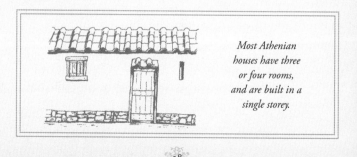

Most Athenian houses have three or four rooms, and are built in a single storey.

A Woman's Place

In terms of civic rights, Athenian women are scarcely any better off than slaves. Upon marriage, they pass from the control of their fathers to that of their husbands. While the women of the poorer classes are often obliged to go out and work, the women of the better classes are forbidden to leave their marital or parental home, and spend their time in the *gynaikeion*, or women's quarters, which are usually on the second floor of the house, far from prying eyes. If Athenian women do appear in public, they are expected to behave with the utmost discretion and to cover their heads and veil themselves with their *himatia*. As bearing children is the main duty of the Athenian wife, a husband is sure to divorce an infertile woman. Although a man may easily repudiate his wife, it is very difficult for a woman to obtain a divorce.

THE HIGH LIFE

In the better class of house, the rooms at ground level open onto a central courtyard. The ground floor has public reception rooms, a private dining room, study, a separate kitchen and a bathroom. The bathroom is often built in a narrow room created by a partition on one side of the kitchen that also serves as a chimney-flue. The bathroom is equipped with a hipbath or a raised basin. An internal staircase leads to the upper floor, which serves as the sleeping accommodation and the women's quarters. The internal decoration is simple: walls are painted in a solid colour – red is often preferred – and floors are tiled. Only in the most luxurious of houses will you find frescoes and mosaic floors. Furniture is sparse, plain and functional: chairs, low tables, beds and storage chests. The only non-functional items are the richly painted vases, which are often given as wedding gifts.

AGRICULTURE AND INDUSTRY:
GIFTS OF ATHENA

ATTICA IS ONE OF GREECE'S LEAST FERTILE REGIONS. THE COMBINATION OF POOR SOIL, MOUNTAINOUS TERRAIN AND DROUGHT MAKES IT UNSUITABLE FOR GROWING CEREALS, AND MOST FRUIT OR VEGETABLES. THE TWO CROPS THAT ARE BEST SUITED TO THE REGION ARE THE VINE AND THE OLIVE, WHICH ARE STAPLES OF BOTH THE ATHENIAN DIET AND EXPORT TRADE. HORSES AND CATTLE DO NOT PROSPER HERE, BUT CONDITIONS ARE SUITED TO THE HARDIER DONKEYS, MULES, SHEEP AND GOATS. TO MEET THE EVER-GROWING DEMAND FOR GRAIN, ATHENS HAS TO LOOK ACROSS THE SEA.

The large landed estates of the nobility have all been broken up in the past hundred years, and the land is now divided into smallholdings among the free citizenry. Despite its great trading reach and industrial production, Attica remains a province of small cultivators, the majority of whom live off the produce of their land. Though many citizens live in the country, farming for a living with the help of no more than one or two slaves, and only come to the city to take part in the Ekklesia, others, who prefer to live in the city, entrust the care of their estates to stewards.

VINE, OLIVE AND FIG

Corn and barley, which are the staples of the Athenian diet in the form of bread and porridge, are grown on the plains of Marathon and Eleusis, but the local production is insufficient to meet the demands of the population. Hence cereals have to be imported from Egypt, Thrace and the Black Sea colonies (see box).

The fruits that Attica is best suited to are the grape, both for

The mountainous scenery of Attica makes it best suited to hardy crops such as grapevines and olive trees.

BLACK SEA GOLD

A major headache for the Athenians is the assurance of a regular grain supply. The pursuit of 'food security', especially in times of war, has engaged Athens in many overseas adventures: in Egypt, in the Black Sea region, and now in Magna Graecia. The supplies from the Black Sea are considered to be the most dependable; hence Athens has seized control of the grain route by establishing colonies and tributary states along the Thracian coast, Propontius and Bosphorus, and by direct action in the Black Sea itself.

the table and to make into wine, and the fig, which is eaten fresh or dried. But the greatest gift of Athena is the olive, which is pressed to make oil. Olive oil and the rich, musky Attic wine are both much sought after and exported widely in earthenware amphorae. While many vegetables are imported from neighbouring states, and are considered luxuries, the Athenians grow their own cabbages, lentils, onions and garlic.

ANIMAL HUSBANDRY

Horses are needed for the army, and cattle for sacrifice to the gods

– especially during the annual Panathenaic festival (see pp. 102–3) – but few are raised in Attica, which has little pastureland. Like corn, they have to be imported from friendly states.

For transport and ploughing, the Athenians use donkeys and mules. The most plentiful and cheapest domesticated animal that is raised for its meat is the pig, and a suckling pig can be purchased for three drachmas (around a day and a half's average wage). Sheep and goats thrive in the poorer upland regions where crops cannot be grown.

AGRICULTURE AND INDUSTRY: CITY OF CRAFT AND TRADE

IT IS NO ACCIDENT THAT ONE OF THE MAJOR ASPECTS OF THE GODDESS HONOURED IN ATHENS IS HER PATRONAGE OF THE CRAFTS AS ATHENA ERGANE, WHOSE SHRINE IS TO BE FOUND ON THE ACROPOLIS. RICH IN DEPOSITS OF FINE CLAY, ATHENS HAS LONG BEEN ONE OF THE MAIN CERAMIC PRODUCTION CENTRES IN GREECE. OTHER WELL-ESTABLISHED TRADES INCLUDE METALWORK, CARPENTRY AND LEATHERWORK, WHICH PRODUCE WARES FOR BOTH DOMESTIC USE AND EXPORT. BUT ATHENS' WEALTH IS DUE IN LARGE MEASURE TO HER THRIVING COMMERCIAL EMPIRE.

Even for the modern-day Athenian who is used to the idea of salaried work, the ideal condition for the freeborn citizen is that of the self-sufficient farmer. Let the metic and slave be dependent upon another man for his bread. With the scarcity of land and a large urban population, however, Athens needs paid work for its citizens. In addition to beautifying the city, the Periklean building programme that began some three decades ago continues to provide much-needed employment for both skilled and unskilled Athenian workers.

CLAY AND METAL

The two crafts in which Athens excels are pottery and metalwork. There are large numbers of potters established in the district

of the Inner Kerameikos. They produce both functional wares such as storage containers, amphorae, cooking pots, braziers, lamps and baths; and high-quality decorative wares (see box), which are exported all over the world.

The smiths of Athens are to be found around the Kolonos Agoraeios, in the shelter of the temple of their patron, the god Hephaistos. The city's bronzesmiths are famous for the quality of their statues, which are made in parts by the lost-wax process. Once its parts are cast, the statue is assembled by brazing, the joins hidden by hammering, and the statue polished to give it the sheen of tanned, oiled skin. The eyes are inset with glass and glisten with semi-precious stones.

THE POTTER'S ART

Athenian ceramics are admired as the finest in the Greek world. In the most ancient times, the Athenians, like the other Greeks, decorated their pottery with geometric designs. Around two centuries ago, they adopted black-figure ware from their Corinthian neighbours, and decorated their pottery with motifs of scenes of daily life, the heroes and gods, and athletic contests. In the last century, the potter Andokites invented red-figure wares, inverting the ground and decoration, which allowed for much greater naturalism and movement in the representation of the figures. Now the work of named vase painters is much in demand for use in *symposia*, as decoration and wedding gifts, and as prizes for athletics contests.

Athens is best known for its red-figure wares.

ATHENS' LIFEBLOOD

Without its dominance of maritime trade, Athens would quickly perish. Not only does Athens need to export her industrial production and surplus oil and wine abroad and to import the grain and raw materials that she lacks, but she also profits as an agent of international trade.

In the present day, the port of Piraeus (see pp. 78–81) has eclipsed its main rivals, Corinth and Aegina, and now dominates trade between Greece and her neighbours. Goods are carried in large merchant vessels, which are known as 'round ships' because they are heavier and broader than the light, shallow-draft military triremes.

Since Athens took command of the seas after the battle of Salamis, merchant shipping is safe from both piracy and the attacks of hostile powers.

MILITARY LIFE:
WARRIORS OF ATHENA

ATHENS HAS NO STANDING ARMY. IN TIME OF WAR, IT IS THE DUTY OF EVERY CITIZEN AND METIC TO COME TO THE DEFENCE OF THE CITY. ALTHOUGH IN ANCIENT TIMES ATHENS, LIKE OTHER GREEK CITIES, DEPENDED IN LARGE PART ON HER HOPLITES, IN HER WARS AGAINST THE PERSIANS AND THE SPARTANS IT WAS HER 'WOODEN WALLS' — HER FLEET — THAT BROUGHT HER SECURITY AND VICTORY.

War is built into the Greek way of life. They fight for honour and for land and scarce resources, but also for the love of fighting. Left to their own devices they will fight one another, but if faced with an external foe, they will unite to deal their common enemy a fatal blow.

Traditionally, Greeks, including the Athenians, fought on land with hoplite heavy infantry, light

ATHENS' 'WOODEN WALLS'

The Athenian navy can muster a fleet of over 350 triremes, each captained and maintained for a year by a leading Athenian citizen. Powered by three banks of oars and two sails, the trireme is both fast and manoeuvrable, even when there is no wind.

It is crewed by 200 freeborn men, 170 of whom man the oars, while the remainder attend to the rigging and steer the twin rudders.

For armament, the trireme has a metal-tipped ramming prow just at the waterline, which is used to hole enemy vessels.

infantry and *hippeis*, or cavalry. Among the Greeks, the militaristic Spartans are acknowledged to be the greatest land fighters.

The war with Persia, however, changed the balance of power in Greece and transformed Athens from one city-state among many into a powerful seaborne force.

LUCKY STRIKE

The Persian War had already been going for a dozen years when Athenian miners struck a rich vein of silver at Laureion (see p. 88). It was up to Themistokles to persuade the Ekklesia that the best use for the money was not to divide it among themselves or erect stronger fortifications around the city, but to trust Athens' defence to her 'wooden walls', that is, to build and equip a fleet of 200 triremes.

Themistokles foresaw that the control of the Aegean would be of vital importance in checking a Persian invasion. Later Athenian leaders, including Perikles (see p. 17), kept to his vision by strengthening the fleet and building major naval facilities at Piraeus. Armed with her navy, Athens has been able to defeat the Persians, build an empire, and hold the Spartans at bay.

MEN OF WAR

The Athenian land forces are made up of light and heavy infantry and cavalry. All citizens reaching the age of 18 have to complete two years of military training known as the *ephebia*. Once this is over, they are liable to be called up for duty at any time.

As citizens buy their own arms and armour, the Athenian army has no standard uniform. The hoplite's armour consists of a bronze breastplate, helmet and greaves. He carries an *apsis* (a large, round shield) that he can sling from one shoulder, and is armed with a *doru* (a long spear) and a *xiphos* (sword). The light infantryman wears less armour, and carries a short spear, javelin or bow. Since the time of Perikles, Athens has maintained a cavalry strength of 1,200 hippeis, armed with javelin, sword and bow.

The military establishment is under the command of the ten *strategoi*, or generals, one from each tribe, who hold office for one year. Unlike other officials who are chosen by lot and cannot hold office in consecutive years, the strategoi are elected and can hold office indefinitely.

An Athenian hoplite's shield stretches from his neck to his thigh, and protects both himself and the man fighting next to him from missiles and in hand-to-hand fighting.

2

THE CITY
OF ATHENS

Athenai, as the Greeks themselves know Athens,
is actually a plural, reflecting the fact that this is a city
of many faces with much to offer any visitor. As well as
the sacred precincts of the 'High City', you may wish to
witness democracy at work in the Pnyx, hear a case
pleaded in the court of the Heliaia, catch a show at the
theatre of Dionysos, or join in with the commercial
hustle and bustle of the Agora.

AN OVERVIEW OF THE CITY

IF YOU STAND ON THE EMINENCE OF THE ACROPOLIS, YOU WILL
SEE ALL THAT ATHENS HAS TO OFFER THE VISITOR. TO THE
NORTHWEST, THE MERCANTILE AND INDUSTRIAL QUARTERS
OF THE AGORA AND KERAMEIKOS; TO THE NORTH AND EAST
THE WEALTHIER RESIDENTIAL QUARTERS; TO THE SOUTHEAST
AND SOUTH, THE MORE CROWDED POPULOUS DISTRICTS; AND
TO THE SOUTHWEST AND WEST, THE WOODED SLOPES OF THE
TWO HILLS THAT ARE THE CITY'S ONLY GREEN SPACES WITHIN
ITS WALLS. ATHENS IS A CITY THAT TRULY HAS IT ALL, AND
ANY VISITOR IS SURE TO BE ENTHRALLED BY ITS HERITAGE,
CUSTOMS AND PEOPLE

Although large by the standards of some other cities, the area enclosed within the city walls is quite compact, and by sticking to the main streets a visitor could cross the city in a little more than an hour.

The main landmark of Athens is the imposing rock of the Acropolis, which provides a useful point of reference. A visitor who is lost will do well to note that its long sides face north and south. The main street of Athens, the Panathenaic Way, begins at the western face of the Acropolis and leads through the Agora to the walls of the city.

The walls of Athens have 13 gates, of which the most important are the Dipylon (double gate) and Sacred Gate, which marks the beginning of the Sacred Way to Eleusis and to the rest of Greece beyond. If you follow the walls east, you will see the heights of Lykabettos and reach the unfinished Olympeion.

It is a short walk from the Olympeion to the monuments found on the south slope of the Acropolis, and as you continue to circle it you will come to the hills of the Muses and of the Nymphs, where the Long Walls to Piraeus begin.

The City Eleusinion,
see p. 60.

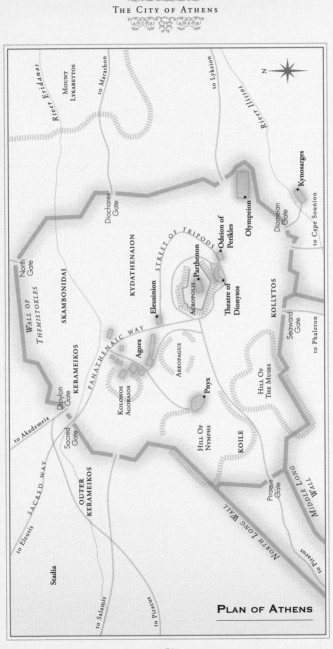

River Eridanos

MOUNT LYKABETTOS

to Marathon

to Lykeion

River Ilissos

N

Kynosarges

Diochares Gate

Olympieion

Dipylaian Gate

Odeion of Perikles

to Cape Sounion

Street of Tripods

North Gate

WALL OF THEMISTOKLES

SKAMBONIDAI

KYDATHENAION

Parthenon

ACROPOLIS

Theatre of Dionysos

KOLLYTOS

KERAMEIKOS

Eleusinion

Seaward Gate

Agora

PANATHENAIC WAY

AREOPAGUS

Pnyx

to Phaleron

Sacred Gate

Dipylon Gate

KOLONOS AGORAIOS

HILL OF THE MUSES

to Akademeia

HILL OF NYMPHS

KOILE

Piraeus Gate

NORTH LONG WALL

MIDDLE LONG WALL

OUTER KERAMEIKOS

SACRED WAY

to Eleusis

to Salamis

to Piraeus

to Piraeus

Stadia

PLAN OF ATHENS

THE ACROPOLIS

THE 'HIGH CITY' OF ATHENS COMBINES SEVERAL FUNCTIONS:
IT IS THE HOLIEST OF SACRED PRECINCTS, WITH SHRINES
AND ALTARS TO THE CITY'S MAJOR GODS; IT IS A TREASURY OF
THE CITY'S RESERVES OF BULLION; AND IT IS THE GREATEST
ART GALLERY IN THE GREEK WORLD, WITH MASTERPIECES OF
SCULPTURE, PAINTING AND ARCHITECTURE. THE CROWNING
GLORY OF THE ROCK, AND OF THE CITY, IS THE TEMPLE
DEDICATED TO ATHENA PARTHENOS, BUT ITS HOLIEST SHRINE
IS THE MORE MODEST TEMPLE OF ATHENA POLIAS.

The steep-sided, walled rock of the Acropolis is accessed by a grooved ramp on its western side. The hill, once sloping from a central crest, has been levelled over the centuries to allow the construction of palaces and temples. Several of its ancient Mycenaean fortifications and terraces remain, incorporated into later buildings, and are a reminder of the antiquity of human habitation on the rock.

Once through the Propylaia, which incorporates the temple of Athena Nike and the Pinakotheke, you face the statue of Athena Promakhos. Immediately to the right are the sanctuary of Artemis Brauronia and the Chalkotheke. A few steps further will take you to the western terrace of the Parthenon. Walking around the south side of the temple past the east porch you will reach the Sanctuary of Pandion. Turning west, you reach the altars of Zeus Polieus and Athena Polias. To the north of the Parthenon, and beyond the foundations of the old temple of Athena, is the Erechtheion. Before

HISTORY OF THE ACROPOLIS

The Acropolis has been occupied since Mycenaean times, when King Theseus' palace stood here. When the Persian invaders drove the Athenians from the city 65 years ago, they desecrated and burned all the sanctuaries on the Acropolis. For 30 years the site remained bare and ruined, until Perikles persuaded the Ekklesia to rebuild it in its present magnificence. The work that began then still continues to this day.

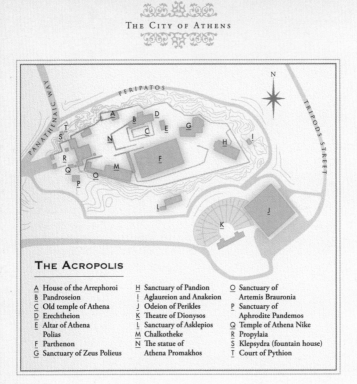

THE ACROPOLIS

A House of the Arrephoroi
B Pandroseion
C Old temple of Athena
D Erechtheion
E Altar of Athena
   Polias
F Parthenon
G Sanctuary of Zeus Polieus

H Sanctuary of Pandion
I Aglaureion and Anakeion
J Odeion of Perikles
K Sanctuary of Asklepios
L Sanctuary of Asklepios
M Chalkotheke
N The statue of
   Athena Promakhos

O Sanctuary of
   Artemis Brauronia
P Sanctuary of
   Aphrodite Pandemos
Q Temple of Athena Nike
R Propylaia
S Klepsydra (fountain house)
T Court of Pythion

regaining the Propylaia, you will pass the house of the Arrhephoroi and the old banqueting hall on your right.

In addition to these major sanctuaries and buildings, you will find a host of votive *stelai* (tablets) and statues all over the rock.

THE SLOPES OF THE ACROPOLIS

The path known as the Peripatos gives you access to the slopes of the Acropolis. Turning right at the foot of the ramp, you come to the court of the Pytheion and the Klepsydra fountain. Follow the path round and you will see many caves and

A plan of the Acropolis showing the major buildings, altars and sanctuaries.

small shrines dedicated to the gods, Athenian heroes and nymphs on the north and east slopes. Once you round the rock to the south slope, you come to the theatre and temple of Dionysos and the Odeion of Perikles. Just beyond stands the sanctuary of Asklepios and Hygieia. Two other important buildings in the vicinity of the Acropolis are the Eleusinion, downhill on the boundary of the Agora, and the Olympeion to the southeast of the rock.

WHAT TO EXPECT

THE SHRINE OF ATHENA HYGIEIA

During the building of the Propylaia, one of the best workers on the project fell from the scaffolding, and his injuries brought him close to death. Athena, as a sign that she approved of the construction, appeared to Perikles in a dream and prescribed a treatment that quickly cured the man. By way of thanks, Perikles dedicated the bronze statue of Athena as Hygieia, goddess of health; it is mounted on a marble base that you can see in front of the southernmost columns of the eastern façade of the Propylaia.

THE PROPYLAIA

To reach the Propylaia, the monumental gateway to the Acropolis built by Mnesikles over a five-year period some 20 years ago, you climb a paved, grooved ramp.

Although it still incorporates parts of the Mycenaean limestone

fortifications, the Propylaia itself is made of lustrous marble from Mount Pentelikon (see p. 97) with a few contrasting elements in darker limestone. Six large Doric columns lead into a deep hall with two rows of three Ionic columns (see p. 45), creating five gateways onto the Acropolis, four with steps for human traffic and one with a ramp for the sacrificial animals.

To the left of the entrance hall is the Pinakotheke, a dining hall with room for 17 couches, which also serves as a painting gallery. To the right is a smaller room, containing a fine statue of Hermes, which leads to the bastion of the temple of Athena Nike (see right).

The marble ceremonial gateway to the Acropolis, the Propylaia, has an extraordinary coffered ceiling.

Although the building has no sculptural ornamentation of its own, it has an extraordinary marble coffered ceiling, decorated with gilded stars on a blue background and featuring floral patterns in gold and other rich colours.

Though magnificent (some may say extravagant, as its main function is as an entrance), the building remains unfinished. The original design includes two further wings that are yet to be built, and some of the marble blocks also remain to be finished.

Like many other buildings in the Periklean programme it includes 'optical refinements' (see p. 45) that harmonise its proportions and strengthen its visual impact.

ATHENA NIKE

The limestone bastion of the temple of Athena Nike, the 'wingless victory', encloses an earlier Mycenaean tower, whose masonry can be viewed through an irregular window opened for this purpose in the base of the wall. The small Ionic temple, finished nine years ago, replaces an older shrine destroyed by the Persians.

The temple has four columns to the front and rear but none to the side. As befits a temple to the goddess of victory, the pediments and the friezes on the rear and sides depict famous battles, such as the battle of Marathon, while the frieze at the front shows an assembly of the gods. The image in the cella, or

inner chamber, is the ancient life-sized wooden Athena Nike that was saved from the Persians. She is holding a pomegranate, a symbol of plenty, in her right hand, and a helmet in her left.

Because the drop from the bastion is precipitous, a waist-high sculpted marble balustrade is currently being built.

The Propylaia incorporates the new temple of Athena Nike.

NIKE

The winged goddess of victory, Nike, is the daughter of the titan Pallas and the River Styx. With her siblings, she is an attendant of father Zeus on Mount Olympus. As decorative and sculptural motifs, many representations of Nike can be seen all over the Acropolis, including votive statues, reliefs and *acroteria*, or roof ornaments. The great statue of Athena Parthenos (see p. 47) holds a solid gold Nike in her right hand.

THE PARTHENON

 ON THE SOUTH SIDE OF THE ACROPOLIS STANDS WHAT THE ATHENIANS CALL SIMPLY, 'TO NEOS' (THE TEMPLE), SUCH IS THE FAME OF THE BUILDING THAT IS ALSO KNOWN AS THE HEKATOMPEDON (HUNDRED-FOOTER) OR THE PARTHENON AFTER THE IMAGE OF ATHENA PARTHENOS (THE MAIDEN) THAT IS ENSHRINED WITHIN IT.

Three things set the Parthenon apart from any other temple yet built in the Greek world: the floor plan, the optical refinements (see right) and the extraordinarily rich decorative scheme.

Commissioned by Perikles as the first building of his programme to restore the Acropolis and adorn the city, the temple took its architects Iktinos and Kallikrates nine years to build. Another six years were needed for the sculptors Pheidias, Agorakritos and Alkamenes to complete the sculptural decoration and to make the marvellous gold and ivory image of the goddess.

Standing on a huge platform of limestone blocks that was built for an earlier, unfinished Parthenon, the Periklean Parthenon is made entirely of Pentelic marble and consists of four parts. The *proneos* is the east porch at the front of the Parthenon. The *Hekatompedon* is the main east room, which contains the cult statue of the goddess. The Parthenon proper, or sacred treasury, is a smaller west room with four interior Ionic columns. And the *opisthodomos* is the rear, western porch.

With its 8 by 17 arrangement of columns, the building serves as

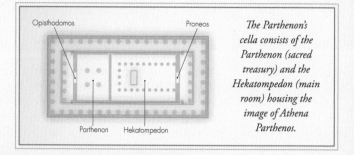

The Parthenon's cella consists of the Parthenon (sacred treasury) and the Hekatompedon (main room) housing the image of Athena Parthenos.

a votive offering to the goddess, the sacred treasury of the city, and the pre-eminent symbol of Athens and Attica. Around the outside is a Doric frieze that consists of alternating *metopes* and *triglyphs*; while a continuous Ionic frieze crowns the top of the cella walls. The two great pediments display life-size images of the gods and scenes connected to Athena.

OPTICAL REFINEMENTS

The Parthenon incorporates a series of 'optical refinements' that harmonise its proportions, increase its impact and make its decoration easier to appreciate.

Your first view of the temple is from the west façade, which has been made a little higher than the east front to make it more impressive. There are few straight lines or right angles in the building. The stepped platform, or *stylobate*, on which the temple stands is not level but curved, and this deviation from the horizontal is reproduced in the entablature. The columns swell and taper, to lighten them and make them appear of equal height and proportion. The columns are in fact not perfectly vertical, but incline very slightly. As a final touch, the blocks making up the friezes are tilted to make them easier to see from the ground level.

Such is the complexity of the design that no two blocks are identical, and all the elements had to be carved in situ.

WHAT TO EXPECT

IONIC OR DORIC?

Many visitors are confused by the two 'orders' or styles of Greek architecture seen in the Parthenon and Propylaia: the Doric and the Ionic. The most obvious differences are in the designs of columns and friezes. You can recognise a Doric column as its shaft rests directly on its stylobate, and it has a plain capital; while an Ionic column has a base – rather than standing directly on the stylobate – and elaborate volute capitals. Above these columns sits an architrave – which is banded in the Ionic style, and plain in the Doric – and upon this is a frieze, which in the Ionic style is continuous, while the Doric consists of alternating metopes (recessed rectangular panels of imagery) and triglyphs (vertical, channelled strips that are raised from the frieze).

DECORATIVE SCHEME

Its Doric exterior gives the Parthenon a severe grandeur, but the temple also boasts of one of the largest and most complex sculptural schemes ever executed in Greece. It took the master-sculptor Pheidias and his two pupils, Agorakritos and Alkamenes, six years to complete the east and west pediments, the Doric and Ionic friezes and the *chryselephantine* (gold and ivory) cult statue of the goddess.

THE PEDIMENTS

The triangular pediments on the east and west faces of the temple are 94 pedes (a Greek foot; see p. 131) long and 11½ pedes high at the apex. Each contains 25 life-sized figures, painted in vibrant colours on a dark blue background.

The east pediment over the entrance to the Hekatompedon shows the birth of Athena from the skull of Zeus, as witnessed by the amazed Olympian gods.

The west pediment shows the competition between Athena and Poseidon for the patronage of the city – Athena, fully armed, stands by her olive tree, her gift to Athens, while Poseidon strikes the rock with his trident; meanwhile, Zeus throws a thunderbolt to prevent his brother and daughter from coming to blows.

METOPES

The entablature of the temple is decorated with a Doric frieze on all four sides. The west side shows the Greeks fighting the Amazons; the north depicts the Trojan War and the sack of Troy; the east features the war between the giants and the gods; and the south, the war between the Lapiths and the centaurs, as well as Athenian heroes and gods.

Like the pediments, the 92 metopes are brightly painted on a blue ground, making them easier to see from the terrace below.

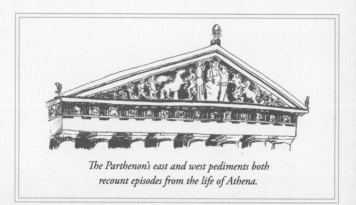

The Parthenon's east and west pediments both recount episodes from the life of Athena.

A Doric frieze of metopes and triglyphs decorates the outside of the temple.

IONIC FRIEZE

The frieze at the top of the cella walls within the *peristyle* (colonnade) is made of 115 blocks creating a continuous narrative stream of the procession of the quadrennial Greater Panathenaia (see pp. 102–3), showing its riders, priests, sacrificial victims and priestesses.

The painted frieze, though tilted outwards, is difficult to see at the best of times, so come when the sun is shining and reflects from the surrounding unpainted marble. The best place to view the frieze from is about 30 pedes from the stylobate on the terrace, though the Doric peristyle still gets in the way.

ATHENA PARTHENOS

Inside the Hekatompedon and framed by a second colonnade is the marvellous statue of the goddess, made of bronze, gold and ivory plates affixed to an armature of cypress and olive wood, which stands a staggering 43 pedes high.

A mind-boggling 42 talents of gold were used to make her *peplos* (robe) and accoutrements. Her helmet is crowned with a sphinx and *pegasoi* (winged horses); her breastplate has the head of the Gorgon Medusa; and her sandals show the war between the Lapiths and centaurs. In her right hand she carries a solid-gold Nike some six pedes tall, and her left hand rests on a shield, showing the war of the gods and giants on its interior, and of the Greeks and Amazons on its face, with the snake Erechthonios (see p. 51) curled up inside.

The statue stands on a base decorated with a depiction of the birth of Pandora, while in front of the statue a pool of water carries the goddess' image and reflects the light from the two windows in the east wall.

The colossal statue of Athena Parthenos in ivory and gold.

THE ERECHTHEION

ALTHOUGH IT IS THE PARTHENON THAT DRAWS THE VISITOR'S
EYE WHEN CROSSING THE PROPYLAIA, IT IS THE SMALLER
ERECHTHEION OPPOSITE THAT LAYS CLAIM TO BEING 'THE
TEMPLE' OF THE ACROPOLIS, AS IT HOUSES THE MOST SACRED
IMAGE OF ATHENA POLIAS (ATHENA OF THE CITY).

The Ionic Erechtheion shows none of the Doric grandeur, symmetry and austerity of its larger neighbour; it is a composite building with a double cella, two porches to the north and south and an enclosure on its west side.

The building of the current Erechtheion, part of the Periklean programme, was interrupted by the Spartan war and is still unfinished. It replaces several earlier temples and incorporates a number of ancient sanctuaries and tombs.

Like the other temples of the Acropolis, the archaic temple of Athena Polias was burned during the Persian sack of the city. However, the ancient image of Athena, said to have fallen from the sky centuries earlier, was evacuated with the population and thus preserved. Before the present temple was finished, the holy statue was housed in the partially restored *opisthodomos*, or rear porch, of the older, ruined temple.

THE EAST TEMPLE

Approaching the temple from the east, you come to an altar of Zeus Hypatos (Zeus most high), on which barley cakes are offered instead of sacrificial beasts. Beyond

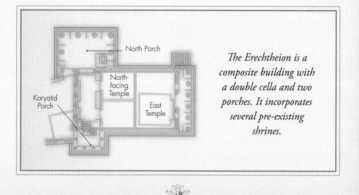

The Erechtheion is a composite building with a double cella and two porches. It incorporates several pre-existing shrines.

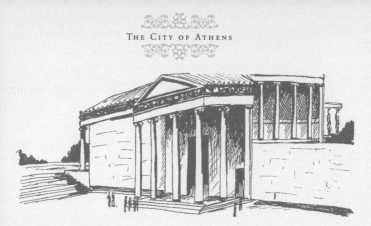

is the portico of six Ionic columns, each 22 pedes high, with elaborate carved and painted capitals.

At the time of writing, an Ionic frieze of the goddess and her attendant priestesses is being carved in white marble against a background of darker Eleusinian stone around the upper walls of the cella.

The east temple contains three altars, all of which stood on the site before the temple was built.

THE NORTH-FACING TEMPLE

Leaving the east temple by the way you came in, take the steps to the right of the porch. You will enter the larger north-facing temple through an impressive Ionic porch to which a frieze is currently being added. The west wall is divided into two: a solid masonry base, and above this four Ionic half-columns with five windows that allow light and air into the interior. This temple houses four of the holiest sanctuaries in Attica, and is full of votive offerings of every kind:

View of the south side of the Erechtheion, with the sacred olive tree given to the city by Athena.

statues, paintings and precious objects in gold and silver. Against the rear wall are the wooden statue of Hermes and the shrine of Athena Polias, which houses her ancient olivewood image and a golden lamp that is kept perpetually alight. The goddess is shown life-sized, wearing a gold crown, earrings and necklaces, holding a solid-gold owl and libation cup, and dressed in the sacred peplos, the elaborate woven gown made by the Arrhephoroi in her honour and presented to her during the Panathenaic festival.

Also displayed here is the larger, sail-sized peplos presented to Athena during the Great Panathenaia. On the opposite side of the room is the salt-water cistern gouged out by Poseidon's trident as he struck the rock, which makes the sound of waves when the south wind blows. To its right is the tomb of Erechtheus.

THE KARYATID PORCH

On the south wall of the north-facing temple is a small porch whose columns take the form of six maidens, or *karyatids*: three stand with their left leg forward, and the other three with the right.

Although the karyatids all look very similar in appearance, you will see that each is slightly different. Each carries a libation cup in her right hand, as if in the act of making a holy offering.

The porch stands over part of the tomb of Kekrops, the first king of Athens, and some suggest that the six maids represent the king's faithful daughters offering the libation to the dead, while others claim that they simply replace the many votive *korai* (see box) smashed by the Persians.

The Karyatids carry libation cups as if in the act of making an offering to the dead.

THE PANDROSEION

At the west end of the temple is the irregular enclosure known as the Pandroseion, named for Pandrosos, daughter of Kekrops. On the northeast corner of the

ATHENA AND POSEIDON

In the time of King Kekrops, Athena and Poseidon vied to become patron of the city. Each offered a bounty to the citizens: Poseidon, a salt-water spring that he caused to gush from the rock, a symbol of the salt sea and its many bounties, and the goddess, the olive tree. The citizens chose Athena's bounty, and the city took her name.

ERECHTHEUS

The temple of the Erechtheion takes its name from King Erechtheus, also known as Erechthonios.

According to legend, Hephaistos was so enamoured of the virginal Athena that he attempted to rape her. The Goddess escaped but his seed fell upon the earth, and Erechtheus, half-man, half-snake, was born. The child was taken by Gaia, the earth, to the Acropolis and given to Athena to raise. She in turn entrusted him, hidden in a basket, to the three daughters of Kekrops: Pandrosos, Herse and Aglauros. Herse and Aglauros were so curious that they opened the basket, went mad when they saw the child, and jumped to their deaths, while the dutiful Pandrosos survived. When he was fully grown, Erechtheus became king of Athens and founded the first temple to Athena Polias.

enclosure is the tomb of Kekrops, part of which is under the Karyatid porch. Immediately to the right is the sacred olive tree – Athena's gift to the city. Although burned by the Persians, it recovered to send up a miraculous new shoot. In the centre is the altar of Zeus Herkeios ('Patron of family ties'). The southwest corner of the enclosure is occupied by the sanctuary of Pandrosos.

WHAT TO EXPECT

KOUROI AND KORAI

Votive wooden and stone statues that represent idealised young men and women were offered to the gods and set up in many sanctuaries and temples.

The statues were carved during the Archaic period and show the influence of Egyptian art. The male figures are always naked, with one leg extended in front of the other in the Eastern manner, while the female figures are always fully clothed. Kouroi and korai are no longer carved and have been superseded by more naturalistic forms of sculpture.

OTHER BUILDINGS
ON THE ACROPOLIS

ALONGSIDE THE PARTHENON AND ERECHTHEION, THE ACROPOLIS IS CROWDED WITH OTHER ALTARS AND SANCTUARIES, AS WELL AS VOTIVE STATUES, STELAI AND BAS-RELIEFS IN WOOD, BRONZE AND MARBLE. A FEW SURVIVED THE PERSIAN DESTRUCTION, BUT MANY ANCIENT CHARRED AND SMASHED IMAGES HAD TO BE BURIED CAREFULLY BEFORE CONSTRUCTION COULD BEGIN AFRESH.

THE BRAURONEION

The origins of the cult of Artemis Brauronia date to the age of the Trojan War, when Iphigeneia brought the statue of the goddess to Attica and established her worship at Brauron. The tyrant Peisistratos, who was a native of the town, brought the cult to Athens.

The Brauroneion is the first building on the right as you exit the Propylaia. In addition to a small temple with an image of Artemis, the enclosure has a Doric *stoa* (portico)

WHAT TO EXPECT

'PLAYING THE BEAR'

The Brauronia festival is held every fourth year. Girls aged from five to ten, known as *arktoi*, 'little she-bears', arrive in procession to serve the goddess as her attendants for one year. They come dressed in saffron robes and as bears – hence the other name for the event, 'playing the bear'. The origins of the festival are explained in a local myth. It is said that a bear that regularly visited the sanctuary became tame because the townspeople fed it. One day a young girl teased the creature, which killed her. Her brother slew the bear, but this so angered the goddess that she demanded that young girls come to her shrine to 'play the bear' in atonement.

for the display of offerings, and votive statues and stelai, including a huge bronze of the Trojan horse with life-sized Greeks peering out. As in Brauron, the Arkteia, the 'playing the bear' rite, is performed here.

SANCTUARY OF PANDION

At the east of the rock is a large open-air enclosure dedicated to Pandion. There were two kings by this name; the Athenians no longer remember which is honoured here, so they pay homage to both. The first was the son of Erechtheus, and the second the son of Kekrops and the father of Aegeus, who, in turn, sired the famous Theseus.

SANCTUARY OF ZEUS POLIEUS

The sanctuary of Zeus Polieus (Zeus of the city) overlooks the north of the Acropolis and is divided into two enclosures: the first has a small temple and altar; while the second provides stabling for the oxen sacrificed during the Bouphonia, or ox-killing festival held in late summer.

The altar is a bronze table on which barley cakes are offered. Oxen are driven around the table until one eats the cakes. The guilty ox is sacrificed with an axe by the *bouphonos* (ox-killer), who immediately drops the axe and runs off. The axe is then tried, cursed and thrown into the sea. The ox is 'resurrected', with its hide stuffed and displayed in the precinct.

WHAT TO EXPECT

SHRINE OF ATHENA ERGANE

The Acropolis had many pre-existing shrines before Perikles commissioned the temples of the Parthenon and Erechtheion. The Erechtheion has its unusual layout because it incorporates several earlier sanctuaries. The Parthenon contains an ancient shrine and circular altar to Athena Ergane within its northern colonnade, though its design was not altered to accommodate it.

ALTAR OF ATHENA POLIAS

Beyond the enclosure of Zeus Polieus is the ancient open-air altar of Athena Polias. It is on a platform reached by a flight of steps. Its sides are decorated with a frieze of the birth of Pandora.

The altar is the focal point of the Panathenaic Festival where the yearly sacrifice to the goddess takes place. Just in front of the altar are the remains of the archaic temple of Athena Polias, destroyed by the Persians, whose ruins are preserved as a reminder.

STATUE OF
ATHENA PROMAKHOS

The first thing you see when you cross the Propylaia is the monumental bronze statue of Athena Promakhos (the champion, or fighter in the forefront), who guards Athens from her enemies.

Pheidias made the statue to celebrate the Greek victories over the Persians. She faces southwest toward Salamis, the site of the war's greatest naval engagement.

The goddess stands some 30 pedes high on a Pentelic marble and limestone base around 15 pedes square. Set in front of the retaining wall of the ancient Mycenaean palace, in good weather her helmet's crest and her

THE PEPLOS OF ATHENA

Every year a new peplos is woven for the statue of Athena Polias, and presented to the goddess during the Panathenaic festival (see p. 102–3). The gown is made by Athenian women, helped by the Arrhephoroi. The peplos is dyed with saffron, with designs woven in purple. Every four years, for the Great Panathenaia, a giant sail-sized peplos is presented to the goddess and displayed in the Parthenon before being taken to the Erechtheion.

An Arrhephoroi and maidens of Athens weave the sacred peplos for Athena.

spearhead can be seen by mariners as they round Cape Sounion. Her shield depicts the war between the Lapiths and centaurs.

The statue, which was begun after the battle of the Eurymedon some 50 years ago, took nine years to complete. Standing close by Athena is a bronze chariot group commemorating a victory against neighbouring Boeotia and Chalkis.

CHALKOTHEKE

Between the Brauroneion and the Parthenon is a walled precinct that is accessed through a propylon known as the Chalkotheke (bronze house), which is said to have been built at the same time as the Brauroneion. It consists of a courtyard and a rectangular building supported by internal columns in which are stored all manner metal objects.

Here you will find not only arms and armour, chariot wheels and axles and naval equipment, but also metal statues, braziers, drinking vessels and lamps – some whole, some broken. Several pieces are displayed in the courtyard.

HOUSE OF THE ARRHEPHOROI

Twenty-five paces to the west of the Erechtheion, set against the northern wall of the Acropolis, you will find the House of the Arrhephoroi, a square building with a single room and a columnar porch facing south. This is the home of the two Arrhephoroi, the attendant priestesses of Athena Polias. Athenian girls aged between six and ten are eligible for the priesthood and serve for one year, during which time they reside on the Acropolis. The Arrhephoroi help in the weaving of the holy peplos (see box). The priestesses begin and end their term of service in the rite of the Arrhephoria, which re-enacts the story of the daughters of Kekrops who were entrusted with the basket containing the infant Erechtheus (see p. 51).

At the end of their year in office, the girls are given sacred objects hidden in baskets that they carry on their heads from the summit of the Acropolis by a secret underground route to reach the sanctuary of Aphrodite below on the north slope. In the lower sanctuary they are entrusted with other objects, also hidden in baskets, which they take back to the Acropolis. On days when the young priestesses have no duties, you can hear the clamour as they play in their own private playground.

THE OLD BANQUETING HALL

The last building on the north side before you return to the Propylaia is the old banqueting hall. However, it is of little interest; it is now used as a storage area since its original function was superseded by the Pinakotheke.

THE SLOPES OF THE ACROPOLIS

A PATH KNOWN AS THE PERIPATOS, WHICH IS IN PLACES NARROW AND PRECIPITOUS, ALTHOUGH IN OTHERS IT IS BROAD AND FLAT, RUNS AROUND THE BASE OF THE ROCK, GIVING ACCESS TO THE SANCTUARIES AND MONUMENTS ON THE SLOPES OF THE ACROPOLIS. ON THE NORTH AND EAST SIDES ARE ANCIENT SHRINES TO THE GODS, HEROES AND NYMPHS, WHILE ON THE SOUTH SIDE YOU WILL FIND MORE SUBSTANTIAL BUILDINGS, INCLUDING THE CITY'S MAIN THEATRE AND CONCERT HALL, AND ALSO THE MAIN SANCTUARY TO ASKLEPIOS, GOD OF HEALING.

THE NORTHWEST SLOPE

Turn right at the base of the ramp to the Propylaia, and follow the broad, paved Panathenaic Way until you reach the fountain house of Klepsydra (literally meaning 'water-thief'), sacred to the nymph Empedo. Inside, water gushes into a carved stone basin from a cleft in the rock. Just beyond the fountain house is the Court of the Pytheion where the ship-shaped cart carrying the giant sail-shaped peplos of Athena Polias for the Greater Panathenaia is parked as the procession continues up the ramp to the Propylaia. Shallow caves above the fountain house contain rustic shrines of great antiquity dedicated to Apollo, Pan and the nymphs.

Although not the focus of great festivals or religious rituals, these sanctuaries are popular with the Athenians and attract many private devotions. Rumour has it that much magic, both black and white, is performed in these ancient precincts.

THE NORTH SLOPE

The Panathenaic Way turns left at the Klepsydra fountain and descends past the Eleusinion to the Agora. The unpaved Peripatos continues straight ahead, hugging the base of the sheer north face of the rock, topped with battlements. Looking up you can see the tiled roof of the House of the Arrhephoroi and the upper part of the Erechtheion. A little way on, a twisting, narrow rock-cut stair leads up to the summit by a small gateway in the defensive enclosure. About halfway along the north side, in a deep cleft in the rock, is the open-air sanctuary of Aphrodite and Eros, with altars, statues of the god and goddess, and niches cut

The slopes of the Acropolis are studded with ancient sanctuaries to the gods and heroes of Athens, situated in clefts and caves in the rock itself.

into the rock face holding votive offerings. An underground passage leads from the sanctuary to the summit, which is used during the rites of the Arrhephoria.

THE EAST SLOPE

The precipitous east slope is devoid of all major constructions, but is the location of two ancient sanctuaries: the Aglaureion and the Anakeion.

The former is a large, deep cave dedicated to Aglauros, daughter of King Kekrops, who threw herself from the Acropolis after opening the basket containing the infant Erechtheus. A series of steps cut into the rock leads up to the mouth of the cave, in front of which stands an altar. Youths of 18 years of age embarking on their two years of military service come to the cave to swear allegiance to the city.

Nearby, a smaller cave houses the Anakeion of the Dioskouroi – the twin demigods who are the protectors of sea-voyages and guests, and also the patrons of horse-racing. The east slope, once considered inaccessible because of the sheerness of the cliff, was left unguarded during the Persian siege of the Acropolis, but the Persians succeeded in scaling it and surprising the defenders from the rear.

THE SOUTHWEST SLOPE

To reach the south slope of the Acropolis, turn left at the base of the ramp. A branch of the Peripatos leads to the foot of the bastion of the temple of Athena Nike (see p. 43), in the base of which are cut two small shrine niches, reproducing similar features in the original Mycenaean tower that the bastion incorporates. A little further along is the sanctuary of Aphrodite Pandemos (Aphrodite of all the people) who represents carnal love, and who is celebrated in the festival of the Aphrodisia.

THE SOUTH SLOPE

Alongside the rock itself and the Agora, the south slope of the Acropolis is one of the most frequently visited areas of the city. Here you will find the main entertainment facilities of Athens and the shrine to Asklepios and Hygieia. The Street of the Tripods, named for the monuments set up by the victorious choregoi of the City Dionysia (see pp. 106–7), begins at the southeast corner of the Acropolis and is one of the busiest thoroughfares of Athens.

THE SANCTUARY OF ASKLEPIOS

About halfway along the southern side of the Acropolis, directly beneath the Parthenon, is a sacred freshwater spring in a small cave.

This was the spot upon which a wealthy private citizen named Telemakhos chose to build the Asklepeion some five years ago. He had gone to Asklepios' main shrine in Epidauros to 'bring back the God' in the form of the snakes that are sacred to him.

Passing through the small wooden propylon, you come to the small temple and altar to Asklepios and his daughter Hygieia. Next to the temple is the Bothros, the stone-lined pit covered with a canopy held up by four columns, where the snakes live. To the right is an Ionic stoa with four rooms that are used for ritual feasting.

ASKLEPIOS

Asklepios is the son of Apollo and the nymph Koronis. He was taught the art of healing by the centaur Chiron. His main sanctuary in Greece is at Epidauros in the Peloponnese. His shrines and temples attract hundreds of pilgrims who come in search of cures (see pp. 138–9).

THE THEATRE AND TEMPLE OF DIONYSOS

Set into the hill next to the Asklepeion is the theatre of Dionysos. Unlike other, less important demes such as Thorikos and Ikarion, the capital city of Attica does not yet have a stone theatre. The *theatron* (seating place) and rectangular *skene* (the all-purpose backdrop behind the *orchestra*, or performance space) are both made of wood. Only the front-row seats, reserved for the priests and state dignitaries, are made of stone.

In spite of its humble form, the theatre has witnessed some of the loftiest dramatic compositions ever staged in the Greek world during the yearly festival of the City Dionysia. In front of the theatre is the ancient sanctuary of Dionysos, with an altar and an archaic temple housing the fine chryselephantine statue of the god by Alkamenes.

THE ODEION

Abutting one side of the theatre is the Odeion of Perikles, a large auditorium some 197 pedes square. The pyramid-shaped roof, said to be modelled on King Xerxes' tent, is supported by ten rows of interior columns, which can make it difficult to see the performances.

The Odeion is used for events that were once held in the Agora, including the *mousikoi agones*, the kithara and flute competitions of the Panathenaic festival, and the *proagon*, the introduction of the plays that are to be shown during the City Dionysia.

Although it is the main performance space in Attica, the theatre of Dionysos has a wooden theatron (seating place) and skene (backdrop).

AROUND THE ACROPOLIS

THE SANCTUARIES OF THE ACROPOLIS, WHILE THEY ARE THE
MOST SPLENDID OF THE CITY, ARE BY NO MEANS THE ONLY
SACRED PLACES IN ATHENS. TO THE SOUTHEAST OF THE
CITY ARE A GROUP OF ANCIENT SHRINES SET AROUND THE
UNFINISHED OLYMPEION, WHILE BETWEEN THE ACROPOLIS
AND THE AGORA LIES THE ELEUSINION, WHICH IS THE FOCAL
POINT OF THE GREATER MYSTERIES OF DEMETER AND KORE
IN ATHENS.

THE CITY ELEUSINION

The City Eleusinion is the
Athenian branch temple of the cult
of Demeter and Kore at Eleusis,
known as the Greater Mysteries
(see pp. 84–5). From the Acropolis,
turn right at the foot of the ramp
and follow the Panathenaic Way
towards the Agora. The temple
stands at the crossroads with the
Street of the Tripods.

Founded one hundred years ago to
strengthen the ties between Athens
and Eleusis, the temple, like so
many others, was destroyed by the
Persians. However, it was rebuilt
much earlier than the shrines on
the Acropolis and has since been
enlarged.

The Ionic temple with four
columns to the front and rear
stands within a walled enclosure
accessed by a propylon. The
cella contains ancients statues of
Demeter, Kore (Persephone) and
Iakhos (Triptolemos). It is here that
the 'sacred objects' brought from
the Telesterion in Eleusis are kept
in preparation for the beginning of
the Greater Mysteries.

The Eleusinion is also used
during the three-day festival of
Thesmophoria.

*The small City Eleusinion is
a branch temple of the main
shrine at Eleusis.*

Demeter (with sceptre) and Kore (with torch), a fragment of a votive relief, marble from Rhamnous in Attica.

THE OLYMPEION

Although Zeus, the father of the gods, is worshipped on the Acropolis as well as in other sanctuaries, he has no major temple of his own like those of Athena on the Acropolis or of his brother Poseidon at Sounion (see pp. 86–7).

The tyrant Peisistratos sought to remedy this oversight by building a great temple to Zeus to the southeast of the Acropolis that would have been larger than the present Parthenon. The temple was begun and completed up to its column bases; however, when the tyranny was overthrown a little under a century ago, the project was abandoned, because the new rulers of the city thought it symbolic of autocratic rule. When the Persians took the city, there was little to destroy, but its stones and columns were later plundered by Themistokles to build the city's walls.

The temple is still unfinished, and its construction will probably have to wait until the completion of the Periklean building programme, which has itself been interrupted by the Spartan war.

PALLADION, PYTHEION AND DELPHINION

In the vicinity of the Olympeion are three ancient shrines that once stood outside the boundaries of Athens before the building of the city's walls. The Palladion is dedicated to Athena as Pallas; the Pytheion, to the Pythian Apollo; and the Delphinion, to Apollo and his twin sister Artemis. In the spring, young girls process to the Delphinion to take part in a festival dedicated to Artemis.

In addition to their religious functions, the Palladion and Delphinion serve as lawcourts for the 51 *Ephetai*, men of over 50 who have served as magistrates and archons. The Palladion hears cases of unintentional homicide and of the murder of metics by citizens; while the Delphinion hears cases of homicide that are claimed to be justified.

THE AGORA

IF THE ACROPOLIS HOLDS ALL THAT IS GRAND AND SACRED IN ATHENS, THE AGORA IS WHERE YOU WILL FIND ALL OF HER RICH AND DIVERSE HUMAN LIFE. HERE ARE THE PUBLIC BUILDINGS THAT HOUSE HER COUNCIL AND SENATE, HER COURTS, AND HER COMMERCIAL EMPORIA, MARKETS, BANKS, PUBLIC FOUNDRY AND WORKSHOPS. BEING ONE OF THE FEW OPEN SPACES WITHIN THE CITY WALLS, IT IS ALSO THE STAGE FOR MANY RELIGIOUS RITUALS, THEATRICAL PERFORMANCES, ATHLETIC CONTESTS, MILITARY TRAINING AND ALL SORTS OF OTHER DISPLAYS.

HISTORY

Unlike the Hippodameia in Piraeus (see pp. 80–1), the Athenian Agora was not carefully planned, but grew with the city's needs. It is thought that the first boundary stones were set up around two centuries ago, although they have since been moved several times. We owe much of the Agora's present layout to the conservative statesman Kimon, who, a little over 50 years ago, planted the plane trees, built the *Tholos* and laid out the *dromos*. Under the stewardship of Perikles, new buildings were added and old ones restored.

To reach the Agora, which means 'meeting place', from the Acropolis, turn right onto the Panathenaic Way and follow it down. The slope begins steeply, but levels out as you reach the first marble *horoi* (boundary stones).

The square nestles beneath the Hill of the Areopagos (see p. 71) and the Kolonos Agoraios topped by the temple of Hephaistos (see p. 68), from which you can get a view of the area. The main civic buildings are on the south, west and north sides, while the east is bordered by shops, workshops and private houses. Starting from the southeast corner, you'll see the mint, the fountain house, the south stoa and the Heliaia. Across Areopagos Street, you will come to the Strategeion, or House of the Strategoi, the Tholos, the Bouleuterion, the Synedrion, the Stoa of Zeus Eleutherios and

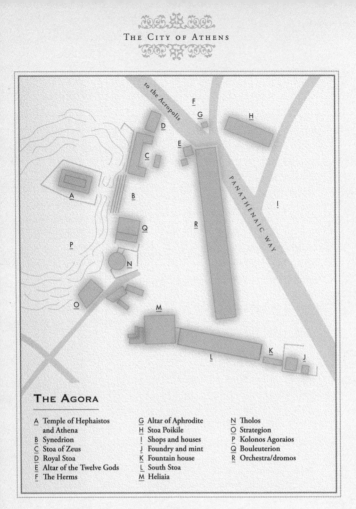

THE AGORA

A	Temple of Hephaistos and Athena	G	Altar of Aphrodite	N	Tholos
B	Synedrion	H	Stoa Poikile	O	Strategion
C	Stoa of Zeus	I	Shops and houses	P	Kolonos Agoraios
D	Royal Stoa	J	Foundry and mint	Q	Bouleuterion
E	Altar of the Twelve Gods	K	Fountain house	R	Orchestra/dromos
F	The Herms	L	South Stoa		
		M	Heliaia		

*The Agora is the political and commercial hub of the city.
Here you will be able to buy foodstuffs, wine, clothing,
manufactured goods and slaves.*

the Royal Stoa. On the north side, beyond the Herms, lies the Poikile Stoa.

The centre of the Agora is occupied by the *dromos* (racetrack) and the *orchestra* (performance space), where civic functions, military displays and athletic and dramatic contests take place. There are also smaller sanctuaries, altars, statues and monuments set in and around the Agora.

THE PANATHENAIC WAY AND THE HERMS

If you are coming from the Dipylon Gate or Sacred Gate along the Panathenaic Way, you enter the Agora from the northwest, past the *horoi* (boundary stones) into the area called 'The Herms' after the many *hermai* that have been set up there.

A herma is a single rectangular stone block with a set of male genitalia and the head of Hermes. You will find them all over the city, placed as boundary markers and for good luck.

To the left of the Panathenaic Way lies the orchestra and dromos, where military displays as well as athletic contests are held; these include the *apobates*, in which men in full armour leap from speeding chariots. The starting blocks for the foot races of the Panathenaic Games are near the Altar of the Twelve Gods, and here you will also see the postholes for the *ikria*, the wooden stands erected for the spectators of the Panathenaia.

The dramatic, dance and music contests of various festivals were held here until they were moved to the theatre of Dionysos and the Odeion.

Herms, or boundary markers, help ward off evil influences.

THE STOA POIKILE

The Stoa Poikile, or 'painted stoa' is the only public building on the north side of the Agora. It looks down the Panathenaic Way towards the Acropolis, and its southern exposure gives it the full benefit of the winter sunshine. The stoa is 41 pedes by 118 pedes with twin colonnades – Doric outside and Ionic inside. The building was made by Peisianax in limestone with marble detailing. It owes its name to the large paintings on

The paintings inside the 'painted stoa' are not to be missed.

sanides (wooden panels) by artists including Polygnotos, Mikon and Panainos. The paintings depict military exploits, including the Athenians fighting the Amazons, the Trojan War, the battle of Marathon and the Athenians fighting the Spartans. In addition to the paintings, bronze shields captured from the Spartans at the Battle of Pylos, just a decade ago, are also displayed.

The stoa has no set function, but is used as a courthouse, a meeting place and for the proclamation of the Eleusinian Mysteries.

THE ROYAL STOA (STOA BASILEIOS)

Across the Panathenaic Way from the Stoa Poikile is the Royal Stoa. At 25 pedes by 60 pedes and with only eight limestone columns, it is the smallest stoa in the Agora.

The building is the office of the king archon, who is in charge of religious affairs and trials for impiety. In front of the stoa are the thrones of the archon and his two assistants, and the Lithos, the stone on which new magistrates swear allegiance.

THE STOA OF ZEUS ELEUTHERIOS

Next to the Royal Stoa stands the grandest of the stoas of the Agora, dedicated to Zeus Eleutherios (Zeus the Liberator). The Doric stoa made by Mnesikles, architect of the Propylaia, has a double colonnade and two projecting wings, and a façade made entirely of costly Pentelikon marble. Before it stands a statue of Father Zeus.

Like the Stoa Poikile, it is decorated with sanides, depicting the Olympian Gods, King Theseus, the personification of Democracy and the shields of slain Athenian warriors. Though primarily a religious building, the stoa also hosts a number of civic and judicial functions.

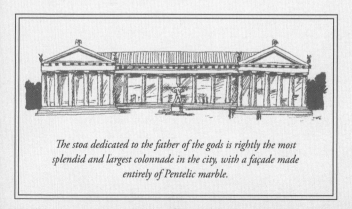

The stoa dedicated to the father of the gods is rightly the most splendid and largest colonnade in the city, with a façade made entirely of Pentelic marble.

THE SYNEDRION

Just beyond the Stoa of Zeus, set into the flank of the Kolonos Agoraios, is the Synedrion, which consists of four rows of seats, and can sit up to 200. This is used as an open courtroom and also for other civic meetings.

THE BOULEUTERION

The two buildings on the far side of the Synedrion form the nucleus of Athenian democracy. The first, the Bouleuterion, was built in the last century to accommodate the 500 members drawn from the ten phylai, or tribes, that make up the Boule, the ruling Council of Athens created by Kleisthenes. The Bouleuterion is 75 pedes square, with five Doric columns at the front and five interior columns supporting the tiled roof. The building is quite plain and made of stone, wood and mud bricks. The only decorations are the acroteria in the shape of sphinxes at each corner of the roof.

In addition to hosting the meetings of the Boule, the building houses the state archives. Although the building was wrecked by the Persians, it was quickly rebuilt after the city was freed. The *bouleutai* sit on tiered wooden benches on three sides of the building.

This modest building houses the Prytaneion, the ruling Senate of Athens.

THE THOLOS

Close by is the Tholos, also known as the *skias* (sun hat) because of the conical shape of the roof. The circular building has a diameter of 60 pedes, with six internal columns.

The function of the Tholos is as the Prytaneion, the residence and dining room of the *prytaneis* (senators) who act as the executive committee of the Boule. Although there are 50 prytaneis at any one

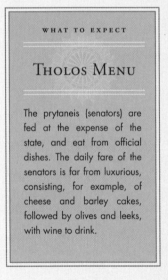

WHAT TO EXPECT

THOLOS MENU

The prytaneis (senators) are fed at the expense of the state, and eat from official dishes. The daily fare of the senators is far from luxurious, consisting, for example, of cheese and barley cakes, followed by olives and leeks, with wine to drink.

The Enneakrounos Fountain House was built by the tyrant Peisistratos for the benefit of the people of Athens.

time, there are only 17 dining couches inside. This is the number of prytaneis that must be in residence in case of an emergency.

The Tholos also contains one of the two sets of official weights and measures on the Agora.

THE STRATEGEION

The last building on the western side of the Agora is the Strategeion, the headquarters of the Athenian army, which is under the command of the third archon, the Archon Polemarch, assisted by ten elected strategoi, or tribe generals.

THE HELIAIA

Once you have crossed Areopagos Street you will reach the large open-air enclosure of the Heliaia, one of the main jury courts of Athens. Its entrance faces north, while on its west side is a colonnade that fronts three rooms, within which the magistrates are able to rest and dine.

THE FOUNTAIN HOUSE

Next to the Heliaia is the South Stoa (see overleaf), and beyond the stoa is the Enneakrounos, 'the fountain house of nine spouts', originally built by Peisistratos.

The fountain house is one of the few places in the city where women may freely gather. You will see them at all times of day filling their *hydria* (water jars) and exchanging the latest gossip.

PUBLIC FOUNDRY AND MINT

The last building on the south side of the Agora is another functional construction, the public foundry and mint where the bronze coins are made, as well as the jury and voting tokens, theatre tokens, and the official sets of weights and measures.

TEMPLE OF HEPHAISTOS AND ATHENA

Overlooking the Agora from the summit of the Kolonos Agoraios is a Doric temple made of Pentelic and Parian marble, dedicated to Hephaistos and Athena. The sculptural scheme mixes Doric elements and Ionic ones, with Doric metopes on all four sides, and Ionic friezes over the front and rear porches.

The carving of the metopes was interrupted by the work on the Acropolis, and only 18 of the 68 planned blocks have been crafted so far, with the others only painted. The metopes depict the labours of Herakles and of Theseus. The front Ionic frieze returns to the deeds of Theseus, which explains the alternative name by which the building is sometimes known: the Theseion. The rear frieze illustrates the war between the Lapiths and centaurs. The front pediment depicts the deification of Herakles as an Olympian god, and the rear, again the Lapiths and centaurs.

As is common among the Greeks, the pediments, friezes and metopes are brightly painted, while the rest of the building is left unadorned. The cella contains bronze statues of Hephaistos and Athena by Alkamenes. Although the cult statues will draw your eye, do not miss the elaborately painted coffered marble ceiling, only rivalled in Athens by the ceiling of the Propylaia.

The temple overlooking the Agora is a double dedication to Athena and Hephaistos.

OTHER SANCTUARIES AND MONUMENTS

In the northwest corner of the Agora is the marble altar of Aphrodite Ourania (Aphrodite the Heavenly). A little to the south is the Leokoreion, a small *abaton*, or enclosed open-air sanctuary, dedicated to the daughters of Leos, who were sacrificed to save the city from the plague, and the triangular sanctuary of Hekate, which has stood for over two centuries. Both enclosures and the nearby public well are full of small offerings left by passers-by. Between the Stoa of Zeus and the Panathenaic Way is the altar to the Twelve Gods, which is both a place of asylum and the centre of the city from which all distances are measured.

Standing to one side of the orchestra south of the altar of the Twelve Gods is the statue of the Tyrannicides. Just under a century ago, two aristocrats, Harmodios and Aristogeiton, killed the brother of the tyrant Hippias on the Agora. The two were executed, but while their quarrel was a private one, they were vaunted as national heroes by the democrats who overthrew the tyranny shortly after.

The present statue by Kritios replaces an earlier statue taken by the Persians. If you're interested in military history you should also take a look at the marble trophy to Miltiades, the hero of Marathon.

COMMERCIAL AND INDUSTRIAL ACTIVITIES

In addition to its civic and religious functions, the Agora is also the main marketplace of Athens, as well as an important industrial production centre. The area east of the Panathenaic Way is occupied by private houses, shops and workshops; the Kolonos Agoraios has iron and bronze foundries.

When there are no military displays or festivals, much of the Agora is occupied by the stalls of merchants.

The South Stoa, between the Heliaia and the fountain house, is a plain, functional building made of stone and mud brick with a single Doric colonnade. The building has 16 rooms, whose doorways are positioned off-centre to allow for the placement of an extra dining couch inside.

It is here that you'll find the city's bankers and moneychangers, in case you need to change foreign currency for Athenian 'owls'. The stoa also houses the offices of the *metronomoi*, the inspectors of weights and measures.

The market of the Agora is divided into several smaller markets, the liveliest of which is the daily fish market.

AROUND THE AGORA

ATHENS IS A CROWDED CITY OF NARROW STREETS WITH LITTLE OPEN SPACE. THE AGORA IS USUALLY PACKED WITH OFFICIALS, JURORS, SOLDIERS, SHOPPERS, MERCHANTS AND IDLERS. BUT TO THE SOUTHWEST OF THE CITY YOU WILL FIND SOME RESPITE ON THE HILL OF THE MUSES AND, WHEN THE EKKLESIA IS NOT IN SESSION, ON THE HILL OF THE NYMPHS. AS AN ADDED BONUS, THESE EMINENCES, ALONG WITH THE HILL OF THE AREOPAGOS, PROVIDE UNRIVALLED VIEWS OF THE CITY, MOUNTAINS AND SARONIC GULF.

HILL OF THE MUSES

If you are feeling oppressed by the heat or business of the city, take a walk away from the madding crowd in the company of poets and philosophers who come to reflect and seek inspiration on the Hill of the Muses.

The gentle climb takes you through scented groves of pine, olive and myrtle, alive with birdsong. The view from the hill is particularly fine. To the south you can follow the line of the Long Walls (see p. 39) to Phaleron and Piraeus and the Saronic Gulf beyond; and to the north, a view of the west and south slopes of the Acropolis, showing the Propylaia, the statue of Athena Promakhos, and the Parthenon to best effect.

HILL OF THE NYMPHS

To the right of the Hill of the Muses, across the road that leads between the Long Walls to Piraeus, is the Hill of the Nymphs, where the Ekklesia meets in a natural stone amphitheatre that is known as the Pnyx.

In the earliest days of the democracy, the Ekklesia met in the Agora, but when this became too crowded, meetings were moved to the nearby Hill of the Nymphs. Set in agreeable parkland,

A walk on the Hill of Muses will refresh even the most jaded of traveller's mind and body.

ATTENDING THE PNYX

Although the Ekklesia decides the fate of Athens, it is not always easy to persuade enough citizens to abandon their business to attend regular meetings when no important affair of state or foreign emergency is on the agenda.

When the Ekklesia is called, the acting prytaneis instruct the Scythian slave archers, who are Athens' police force, to block off the streets leading to the Agora and use a rope covered in red dye to corral and lead the citizens firmly towards the Pnyx. Anyone found to have his clothes stained by the dye is liable to a fine.

The session begins with a sacrifice to the gods, and the victim's blood is smeared around the Pnyx, signifying that it has become a sacred precinct. Then the president of the Ekklesia announces the day's agenda, which he asks those present to approve. He then invites the citizens to come forward and speak with the words, 'Tis agoreyein bouletai?' ('Who wishes to speak?').

Votes are taken by a simple show of hands, and measures passed have the strength of law unless struck down as being unconstitutional by the courts.

the Pnyx can accommodate some 6,000 citizens quite comfortably, which constitutes a quorum of the Ekklesia, but it is said that up to 20,000 can find a place there if the need arises.

The *bema*, or speaker's platform, used to face northwest, so that the people looked towards the sea, but latterly the direction of the bema has been reversed so that the people now face northwest, with the Acropolis on their right. The prytaneis, whose job it is to oversee the sessions, sit in wooden chairs, while most citizens either stand or sit on the ground, terraces and retaining walls.

HILL OF THE AREOPAGOS

Take Areopagos Street from the Agora and you will reach the Hill of the Areopagos.

Before the democracy, the rock was the meeting place of the Council of the Areopagos, which acted as Athens' supreme court and senate. The hill offers good views over the Agora, and of the Acropolis.

SURROUNDING
AREAS

You may think that once you've visited Athens,
with its grandiose temples and bustling Agora, you've
seen all that Attica has to offer. But think again.
Starting with the immediate environs of Athens, the
demes of Attica hold many sites – natural and
manmade – to delight the heart, calm the mind and
elevate the spirits. If it's crowds, markets and shopping
that you seek, then head for the cosmopolitan emporion
of Piraeus; if it's grandeur and mystery, take the
Sacred Way to the Telesterion of Eleusis; and for
natural beauty, scale the heights of Mount Parnes or
look out to sea from the headland of Sounion.

ATHENS BEYOND THE WALLS

THE IMMEDIATE ENVIRONS OF THE CITY PRESENT MANY CONTRASTS FOR THE VISITOR. 'THE LEGS', AS THE LONG WALLS ARE KNOWN, LEAD TO THE BUSY PORT OF PIRAEUS AND THE SANDY BAY OF PHALERON, BUT IF THE (MALE) VISITOR PREFERS TO REFRESH HIS MIND AND EXERCISE HIS BODY, HE CAN USE THE FACILITIES OF THE CITY'S THREE FINE PUBLIC GYMNASIA: THE AKADEMEIA, THE KYNOSARGES AND THE LYKEION.

Leaving the city by the Piraeus Gate, you will reach the enclosed area within the northern and middle long walls, a massive system of defensive fortifications some 162 *stadia* long. A third, southern wall, now fallen into disuse, links the city to the port of Phaleron (see p. 86).

Ta skele, or 'the legs', is the nickname given to the long walls that link the city to the port of Piraeus within a single continuous defensive enclosure. Initially the Ekklesia decided to build two walls, a northern wall to Piraeus (see pp. 78–81) and a shorter southern wall to the ancient port of Phaleron. The walls enclosed a triangular wedge of land with Athens at its apex and Phaleron Bay at its base.

The walls were completed a little over 40 years ago in spite of a Spartan invasion intended to prevent their construction. A decade later, Perikles persuaded the Ekklesia to build a third, middle wall, parallel to the north wall,

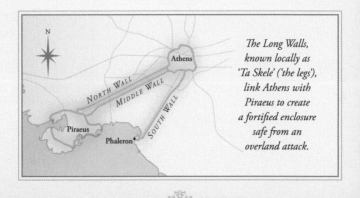

The Long Walls, known locally as 'Ta Skele' ('the legs'), link Athens with Piraeus to create a fortified enclosure safe from an overland attack.

LYKABETTOS HILL

If you are looking for views over the city, climb Lykabettos Hill to the northeast of the city. Lykabettos – meaning 'where the wolves walk' – owes its name to the wolves that once lived there, though hunting has since destroyed the population.

The hill is a sheer plug of limestone with a bare summit and pines around its flanks, and is the highest point on the plain of Athens. On reaching the summit, the climber will be rewarded with exceptional views over the north side of the Acropolis, the city and the Saronic Gulf beyond.

creating a fortified corridor to Piraeus. He appointed Kallikrates, one of the architects of the Parthenon, to build it.

With the city and its access to the sea protected by the long defensive walls, Athens cannot be forced into submission by siege. Although the Spartans invade and ravage the countryside every year, they cannot starve the city because it can be re-supplied by sea. Perikles decided that Attica's people should shelter within the defensive enclosure he had created, greatly increasing the population of Athens and Piraeus.

Although the people were safe from Spartan attacks, the crowded conditions led to the outbreak of a plague that killed one third of the city's population and claimed Perikles himself.

OUTER KERAMEIKOS CEMETERY

If you leave the city through either the Dipylon Gate or the neighbouring Sacred Gate you will enter the main cemetery of Athens. Among the many ancient and modern tombs, each marked with a grave marker, shrine or monument, you will find the Demosion Sema, the public cemetery dedicated to the men who have fallen in the service of Athens. Here are also thousands of victims of the plague that struck Athens some 15 years ago.

Some two stadia from the Dipylon Gate in the direction of the Akademeia (see overleaf), you will pass the ancient shrine of Artemis, with its fine wooden statues of the goddess as Ariste and Kalliste.

THE GYMNASIA

Athens itself has three publicly maintained gymnasia outside the city walls: the Akademeia, Lykeion and Kynosarges. In addition to providing sporting facilities for the male residents of Athens, the gymnasia are used for military training and exercises, and they are also the site of ancient sanctuaries and religious festivals.

THE AKADEMEIA

The Akademeia (Academy) is the furthest of the three gymnasia from the city. From the Dipylon Gate, follow the broad Dromos six stadia through the Outer Kerameikos to reach the grove named for the hero Akademos.

In addition to the *palaestra*, or wrestling ground, and *dromos*, or racetrack, the walled gymnasium of Akademeia is adorned with statues, sanctuaries and the graves of famous Athenians.

The shady gardens, watered by the Kephisos River, are a favourite walking spot for citizens. Here you will find one of the most hallowed and ancient groves sacred to Athena, which contains the 12 *moriai*, olive trees grown from the seeds of the sacred tree in the Erechtheion. The oil pressed from their fruit is given as the prize for the victors in the Panathenaic Games.

There are also altars to Hermes and Eros and one to Prometheus, which is the starting point of an annual night-time torch race dedicated to the titan who gave fire to mankind.

THE LYKEION

Located to the east of the city, just beyond the Diochares Gate, near the source of the Eridanos River and the fountain of Panops, the Lykeion (Lyceum) owes its name to the sanctuary of the Lykeian (wolf) Apollo, this animal being sacred to the god.

In addition to a palaestra, the gymnasium has a dromos, which measures two stadia. Not far from the Sanctuary of Apollo, you will find sanctuaries to Hermes and the Muses. A nearby stoa displays maps of the known world on its walls.

This is said to be the favourite palaestra of Sokrates, who is often found here admiring the athletes as they train, or deep in conversation with fellow philosophers.

KYNOSARGES

The third of the public gymnasia is located a little way from the Diomeian Gate to the southeast of the city on the south bank of the River Illissos. It is famous for its sanctuary dedicated to Herakles, his mother Alkmena, his wife Hebe and his companion Iolaos.

Kynosarges is the site of the Herakleia, a yearly sacrifice and festival held in honour of the hero.

WORKING OUT THE ATHENIAN WAY

The gymnasia are equipped with running tracks, training grounds, horse and chariot racetracks, baths, and also shops selling the supplies needed by athletes.

A stlengis used by athletes for removing dirt and oil; the curve allows it to fit the contours of the body.

All freeborn men are entitled to train at the publicly maintained gymnasia, be they citizens or metics. The main training facility is an open area with a colonnaded lobby with benches on one or two sides where the athletes change and rest.

It is the custom to exercise naked, with the body oiled and sprinkled with fine sand to ward off the chill. After limbering up and digging over the ground to soften it, athletes train in the six major sports: wrestling, running, javelin, discus, long-jump and *pankration* (a brutal no-holds-barred version of bare-knuckle boxing), all accompanied by the sound of the resident musician playing the *aulos*, or flute. Once his training is over, the athlete scrapes the oil, sand and dirt from his body with a *stlengis*, or scraper, and takes a bath.

PIRAEUS

PIRAEUS IS SO IMPORTANT TO THE SURVIVAL OF ATTICA THAT THE EKKLESIA ONCE CONSIDERED ABANDONING THE CITY OF ATHENS ITSELF IN FAVOUR OF ITS ASSOCIATED PORT. LUCKILY FOR THE WORLD, THE PLAN WAS NEVER CARRIED THROUGH. ALTHOUGH IT IS CLOSELY TIED TO ITS INLAND SISTER, PIRAEUS IS A LARGE, BUSTLING, COSMOPOLITAN METROPOLIS IN ITS OWN RIGHT. IT IS THE SECOND LARGEST CITY IN ATTICA, AND AS SUCH IT CAN BOAST OF BEING GREECE'S MAIN COMMERCIAL AND NAVAL PORT.

If you are coming from Athens, exit from the Dipylon Gate and walk along the two-lane road outside the northern long wall. The distance of 50 stadia will take you two to three hours depending on the traffic. In times of hostilities, however, you will have to travel within the cramped confines of the long walls, which will be crowded with carts bringing provisions to the city and soldiers going to and from their posts.

Travellers arriving from overseas will most likely arrive by boat at Kantharos (see p. 80), the main civilian harbour, and visitors from other parts of Attica – especially other coastal communities – often choose to travel there by ship rather than trust to the terrible roads. Ferries depart from Piraeus bound for the neighbouring islands, including Aegina and Salamis, as well as towns farther down the coast, for an average fare of 1–4 obols (an obol is worth 1/6 of a drachma).

LAY OF THE LAND

With an estimated population of some 30,000, the Attic deme of Piraeus is built on a rocky limestone peninsula 20 stadia long overlooking the Saronic Gulf.

The fortified town is built around three superb natural harbours that have been improved by building additional sea defences. The city occupies a central isthmus enclosed between two raised masses: Mounychia Hill and the Akte Plateau.

ENTERTAINMENT

Piraeus boasts four principle festivals: the Asklepieia, which is dedicated to the god of healing;

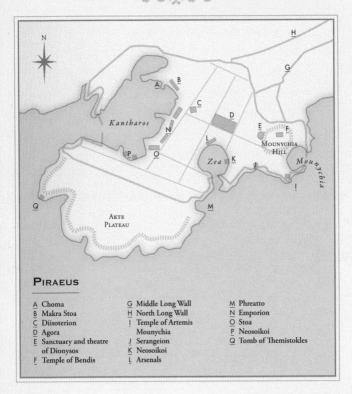

PIRAEUS

A Choma
B Makra Stoa
C Diisoterion
D Agora
E Sanctuary and theatre of Dionysos
F Temple of Bendis
G Middle Long Wall
H North Long Wall
I Temple of Artemis Mounychia
J Serangeion
K Neosoikoi
L Arsenals
M Phreatto
N Emporion
O Stoa
P Neosoikoi
Q Tomb of Themistokles

the Bendideia, in honour of the Thracian goddess Bendis, which is celebrated with torchlit races on horseback; the Dionysia, with its associated dramatic performances; and the all-female festival of the Thesmophoria.

The port of Piraeus is crucial to the people of Attica and Athens. Its pivotal importance is reflected in the defensive fortifications that link it with Athens.

HISTORY

Piraeus became the main port of Athens a little under 70 years ago. Themistokles realised that its three natural harbours and easily defensible position made it much easier to protect than the port of

Phaleron, and he then decided it should be fortified with a defensive wall.

The fortifications of the town were finally completed with the building of the middle long wall that links it to Athens.

GETTING AROUND

It is easy to find your way around Piraeus because its streets are laid out in a grid pattern around the three superb natural harbours: Kantharos, Zea and Mounychia.

KANTHAROS

The Megas Limen or Grand Harbour of Kantharos is one of the largest natural anchorages in the Middle Sea. The entrance has been narrowed to 160 pedes by the construction of two moles between which a chain can be hung to close the harbour to enemy shipping. Two lighthouses mark the entrance, and the tomb of Themistokles stands on the southern approach.

The lion of Piraeus stands at the mouth of the Kantharos.

Kantharos is both a commercial and a military harbour. The naval installations include 94 *neosoikoi*, or ship sheds, on the southern shore and the naval headquarters on the northern shore.

THE FATHER OF TOWN PLANNING

Hippodamos is a native of Miletus in Asian Ionia. He established his reputation in helping to rebuild his native city 64 years ago.

Perikles appointed him to remodel the city of Piraeus, which was already an important naval and commercial port. He devised a grid plan for the town that contrasts with the haphazard layout of Athens, and laid out the agora with its market and civic buildings.

EMPORION

The eastern shore of Kantharos is occupied by the commercial port known as the Emporion. Commercial vessels arrive at the three main *kripidai*, or piers, to unload their cargoes.

Behind the docks stand five stoas used for the display and storage of merchandise. At the northern end is the Makra Stoa, which is the all-important grain market, and in the centre is the Deigma Stoa where samples of imported merchandise are displayed, and where the bankers of the city ply their trade.

Just behind the Emporion is the Diisoterion, the joint temple of Zeus Soter and Athena Soteira ('Saviour'). Once you have visited the temple, walk eastwards until you reach the agora, also known as the Hippodameia in honour of its builder (see left). The agora is the civic centre and marketplace for all goods arriving by land.

ZEA AND MOUNYCHIA

To the south of the agora, you reach the walled area around the war harbours of Zea and Mounychia. The naval installations consist of 272 neosoikoi and several large wooden *skeuothekai*, or arsenals, in which masts, oars, sails and tackle are all stored during the winter months.

Although you may not enter these harbours, you can obtain a great view of them by climbing up Mounychia Hill. On the northwestern side of the hill is the sanctuary of Dionysios and a fine stone theatre, where the dramatic contests of the local Dionysia are held in the winter. Close to the summit, you will come to the sanctuary of Bendis, a Thracian goddess and one of the few foreign goddesses who are worshipped in Attica. The hill offers a fine view of Phaleron Bay and the city of Athens beyond. On the western headland of Mounychia harbour you will find the ancient shrine of Artemis Mounychia, and if you need to refresh yourself after the day's sightseeing, visit the Serangeion, a large circular bathhouse found a little farther along the coast towards Zea.

JUSTICE AT SEA

The court of Phreatto holds its sessions on the eastern side of Zea. This court has jurisdiction over cases involving those who have been ostracised (see p. 19) by a vote of the Ekklesia and are not allowed to return on pain of death. The magistrates and jurors sit on the shore while the exiled claimant pleads his case from a boat anchored just offshore.

ELEUSIS

FOR MANY GREEK VISITORS, THERE IS ONLY ONE REASON TO
COME TO ATTICA: NOT TO SEE ITS FINE BUILDINGS NOR EVEN
ITS ARTISTIC TREASURES, BUT TO BECOME MYSTAI — INITIATES
INTO THE MYSTERIES OF DEMETER AND KORE THAT TAKE
PLACE EVERY YEAR IN ATHENS AND ELEUSIS. ALTHOUGH
INITIATES MUST PARTAKE IN THE LESSER MYSTERIES IN
SPRING, IT IS THE GREATER MYSTERIES THAT STAND AS
ONE OF THE DEFINING FESTIVALS OF GREECE. CELEBRATED
OVER A PERIOD OF NINE DAYS OF RITUAL AND FEASTING,
THESE EVENTS CULMINATE IN A GRAND PROCESSION AND THE
INITIATION INTO THE SECRETS OF THE CULT.

GETTING THERE AND BACK

Eleusis lies some 118 stadia to the west of Athens.

If you are taking part in the procession of the Greater Mysteries (see overleaf), arrive early at the area between the Dipylon and Sacred Gates. Once everyone is assembled, the procession will set off along the Sacred Way through the Outer Kerameikos cemetery. When you reach your halfway point you will pass the shrine of Apollo and the open-air sanctuary of Aphrodite with its rock-cut offering niches. After crossing the Rhetoi Lake on the newly built bridge, and before entering Eleusis proper, you will be ritually insulted by masked men on the road, to remind you to be humble in the presence of the goddesses.

TWINNED CITIES

When Eleusis was incorporated into Attica proper, the Athenians adopted the ancient cult of Demeter and Kore, turning it into one of the most important pan-Hellenic cults of mainland Greece. To strengthen the ties between the two cities, the City Eleusinion was built between the Agora and Acropolis, and the great yearly procession from Athens to Eleusis along the Sacred Way was instituted. Such is the popularity of the Greater Mysteries that it, like the Olympic Games, is the occasion of a sacred truce.

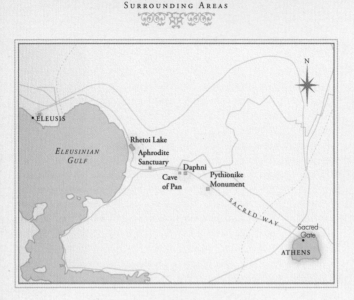

The procession of the Greater Mysteries departs Athens on the Sacred Way, following it west across Rhetoi Lake and finally to Eleusis.

LAY OF THE LAND

The westernmost Attic deme, the city of Eleusis is built on a ridge overlooking the Bay of Eleusis opposite the island of Salamis, south of a broad, fertile plain.

The sanctuary of Demeter and Kore (Persephone) is situated on the eastern side of the acropolis within a walled enclosure that is accessed by a large ceremonial gateway. The main features of the sanctuary are the Kallichoron, or Sacred Well, the cave of Hades found next to the triangular court, and the Telesterion, into which only initiates are allowed to enter.

HISTORY

According to tradition, the cult of Demeter at Eleusis dates back to Mycenaean times. The town was one of the 12 original cities of Attica united by Theseus.

The first cult centre, or Telesterion, was built over three centuries ago and was enlarged first by Solon and later by Peisistratos. This first building was destroyed by the Persians and rebuilt on a grander scale by Perikles. Although much of Attica is currently ravaged by war, the status of Eleusis as a pan-Hellenic sanctuary has made it immune from Spartan attack.

THE SECRET CULT

The festivals of the 'Lesser' and 'Greater Mysteries' are held in spring and fall respectively, and are open to all Greeks, whether male or female, freeborn or slave. However, barbarians and individuals polluted by death or blood are barred. All those wishing to take part in the Greater Mysteries must first attend the Lesser Mysteries.

Although the public rites of the cult are known and will be described below, what takes place within the Telesterion is a closely guarded secret. The penalty for revealing the secret of the Mysteries is death. This makes the Mysteries a unique religious cult in the Greek world, where rituals are otherwise open for all to see.

THINGS SPOKEN, SEEN AND PERFORMED

The Greater Mysteries is one of the three major festivals of the Athenian year (see p. 100) and attracts participants from all over the Greek world.

If you plan to visit Athens for the nine days of the festival, arrive early, as the city will be full and accommodation difficult to find. On 14 Boedromion, the eve of the festival proper, the 'Sacred Objects' are carried in round boxes from Eleusis to the Eleusinion in Athens (see p. 60). The following day, the mystai assemble in the Agora in front of the Poikile Stoa where the *hierophants* (priests) announce the start of the rites. On the 16th, the mystai go to Phaleron Bay to wash themselves and the pigs they are to sacrifice to the goddess. Once they have purified themselves, offered sacrifice and feasted for two days, the mystai assemble at the Sacred Gate on the morning of the 19th.

The procession to Eleusis is led by the wooden statue of Iakhos, son of Demeter and Zeus, followed by the priests bringing back the sacred cult objects, again hidden from view in boxes, and the mystai in high spirits, crowned with myrtle and swinging branches as they walk, crying '*Iakkhe! Iakkhe!*' in honour of Demeter's son. They arrive in Eleusis at nightfall and spend the next day fasting in memory of Demeter's fast when she grieved for her lost daughter.

A wooden statue of Iakhos, the son of Demeter and Zeus, is at the forefront of the procession to Eleusis.

On the 20th, the mystai are ushered into the Telesterion where the Sacred Objects have been returned. All that can be said about this element of the Mysteries is that they consist of 'things spoken, seen and performed'.

Once the initiation is over, the mystai attend an all-night feast with much revelry and dancing. A bull is sacrificed in the early hours, and then later on the 22nd libations are made to the dead. The festival ends on 23 Boedromion.

THE TELESTERION

The most secret rites of the Mysteries take place within the Telesterion, a huge pillared hall that is 180 pedes square, featuring eight tiers of terraced stone benches on each side that can seat up to 3,000 mystai. Inside the Telesterion is a second building, the Anaktoron, or 'palace', the holy of holies of the cult, which is open only to the priests, and in which the sacred cult objects are stored. On the west side of the Anaktoron is the throne of the high hierophant. It is rumoured that at the height of the initiation ceremonies the hierophant emerges from the Anaktoron in a blaze of light, bearing the sacred objects that are then 'shown' and 'spoken of' to the mystai. Beyond this, it is not wise to inquire or to speculate.

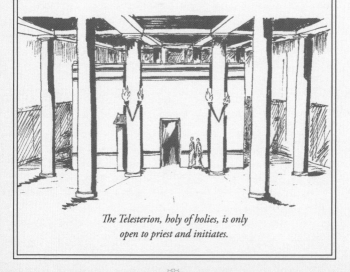

The Telesterion, holy of holies, is only open to priest and initiates.

THE SARONIC COAST

THE SARONIC COASTLINE OF ATTICA STRETCHES FROM PIRAEUS AND PHALERON BAY TO THE PICTURESQUE HEADLAND OF CAPE SOUNION, A ROCKY PROMONTORY THAT OVERLOOKS THE AEGEAN SEA, AND IS GRACED BY THE SANCTUARIES OF THE TWO GODS MOST CLOSELY ASSOCIATED WITH ATHENS: POSEIDON, THE LORD OF THE OCEANS; AND ATHENA, THE PATRON OF THE CITY.

PHALERON

To reach Phaleron, some 16 stadia southwest of Athens, exit through the Phaleron Gate and follow the road running along the disused Phaleronic southern wall.

According to tradition, Theseus sailed to Crete and Menestheus for Troy from Phaleron. Before the development of Piraeus, the Greek fleet was beached in the bay and commercial vessels unloaded their cargoes here for transportation to Athens. Today, Phaleron Bay is busiest on 16 Boedromion, when the mystai of the Greater Mysteries of Eulesis come here to purify themselves and their offerings in the sea.

SOUNION

Although there is an unpaved coastal road, the best way to travel the 362 stadia southeast from Athens to Sounion is to go by sea from Piraeus (fare: 2–4 obols).

The town has a good anchorage and is a landmark for ships coming from the Aegean islands. Climbing to the highest point of

TEMPLE OF ATHENA SOUNIAS

A couple of stadia to the north on a lower hill stands the walled sanctuary of Athena Sounias. Built in the local marble around 35 years ago, it replaces an Archaic temple destroyed by the Persians.

The shrine has an extremely unusual floor plan, with columns only on its east and south sides. The Ionic capitals of the colonnade are particularly finely carved and richly painted. The 12 columns on the southern side create a stoa. Standing close by is a small Doric temple that is dedicated to the hero Phrontis.

TEMPLE OF POSEIDON

The hill on which the temple stands is currently being fortified to protect it from Spartan incursions.

Once inside the walls, you enter the sacred enclosure through a marble and stone gateway. Immediately to the right is a stoa used to display offerings and for ritual feasts. The current Doric temple was built 30 years ago and resembles the temple of Hephaistos in Athens (see p. 68). The temple has an arrangement of six by thirteen fluted columns carved from the handsome local marble. The sculptural decoration depicts the wars of the Lapiths and centaurs and of the gods and giants, a boar hunt, and the deeds of Theseus. Within the temple, the windowless *naos*, or cult room, houses the gilded bronze image of Poseidon, 18 pedes high, showing the god brandishing his trident.

the headland will give good views of the nearby islets of Helena and Patroklos. On a clear day, you will be able to see the Cyclades islands far to the south.

According to legend, it was from the cliffs of Sounion that King Aegeus threw himself into the sea, wrongly believing that his son Theseus had been killed by the Minotaur in Crete. King Menelaus, returning from Troy, also stopped here to bury his helmsman.

The original temple of Poseidon was destroyed during the Persian invasion, but the site was restored in the time of Perikles.

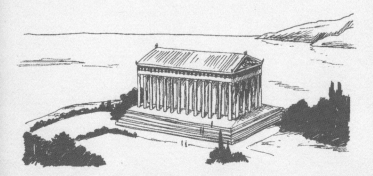

The imposing temple of Poseidon greets the traveller arriving to Attica by sea.

THE EUBOEAN COAST

FROM SOUNION TO THE NORTHERNMOST ATTIC DEME OF RHAMNOUS, THE ATTIC COASTLINE IS SHELTERED BY THE LARGE ISLAND OF EUBOEA, A VASSAL STATE OF ATHENS AND AN IMPORTANT SOURCE OF GRAIN FOR THE CITY. JUST NORTH OF SOUNION ARE THE MINING DEMES OF LAUREION AND THORIKOS, AND HALFWAY UP THE COAST IS THE IMPORTANT SHRINE OF ARTEMIS AT BRAURON.

LAUREION

To reach the Attic mining deme of Laureion, follow the coastline some 40 stadia north of Sounion until you reach the place whose name instills dread in the heart of any enemy of Athens: Laureion. Silver

SILVER MINING

The deposits of argentiferous lead are reached from deep vertical shafts off which radiate cramped, horizontal tunnels. The ore is taken to 'washeries' in Laureion and Thorikos to be separated from the spoil. The ore is then heated in furnaces and the impurities – mainly lead – are removed, leaving behind pure silver to be minted into coins.

– the 'divine bounty' of Athens – is also the curse of its prisoners of war, who are sent in their thousands to work in the mines in conditions that are generously termed 'squalid', and where life is brutish and short.

Some 67 years ago Athens struck a rich vein of silver at Laureion, which enabled her to build the fleet that defeated the Persians at Salamis (see p. 16) and gave the city her empire. The area is pockmarked with 350 mines that produce 1,000 talents of silver annually. The silver is of such purity that Attic 'owls' (see pp. 150–1) – the nickname of Athenian silver coins – are used as the preferred unit of currency for international trade from the cold lands of the Keltoi in the northwest to as far east as India.

THORIKOS

Located 11 stadia north of Laureion, the walled town of Thorikos is built on a hill with two peaks, overlooking a sheltered anchorage on the seaward side and a fertile plain on the landward.

The site was settled in remotest antiquity, as witnessed by the four Mycenaean tombs in the vicinity. The tombs, known as *tholoi*, 'beehive tombs', are conical in shape and buried under earth mounds. The larger tombs are reached through a *dromos*, or entrance hall. All the four tholoi in Thorikos were opened in the distant past, and some of their contents were removed. The locals consider one of the smaller tombs to be a shrine to an unnamed hero, and they leave small offerings when they pass by.

Thorikos has been made rich by the silver mines that are found all over the deme. The city is honeycombed with mineworkings and has many ore-washing and smelting factories. But the town has more to offer to the visitor than just industrial interest.

On the south side of the hill is one of Attica's oldest stone theatres, where the dramatic contests of the Rural Dionysia (see p. 107) take place every winter. Just east of the theatre is the temple of Dionysios and a shrine of the goddess Hygieia. At the foot of the hill is an unfinished Doric stoa began some 15 years ago when Perikles was still alive. The building, dedicated to the goddess Demeter, who stopped here on her way to Eleusis, is built of the local marble. Although

The silver mined in Laureion is extracted and smelted into ingots on site.

unfinished, the peristyle of seven by fourteen columns is of the highest workmanship, albeit with an unusual floorplan, with the central gap that divides the building into two equal halves.

BRAURON

Located 205 stadia southeast of Athens and 44 stadia north of Thorikos, Brauron, along with Eleusis, is one of the most sacred sites of Attica. It is dedicated to the virgin goddess Artemis, goddess of the hunt and, also, perhaps strangely, of childbirth.

The sanctuary was established four centuries ago and is the site of a major festival, the Brauronia, which is held every four years. Like many other temples in Attica, the original sanctuary was destroyed by the Persian invaders, who carried off the cult statue.

In addition to the sanctuary itself, Brauron has a gymnasium with a palaestra.

SANCTUARY OF THE GODDESS

If you have taken the arduous land route from Athens, you will reach one of the few stone bridges in Attica, which crosses the River Erasinos.

Once across the rutted span of the bridge, you will come to the Π-shaped limestone and marble Doric stoa, built, it is said, to ward off the terrible plague of 15 years ago. The unfinished building has nine dining rooms for ritual feasts, each with seven metal couches and stone tables. Behind the dining rooms lies a corridor in which the clothes of women and children who have died in childbirth are displayed. The stoa also houses the many votive dedications that have been offered to the goddess in order to secure a safe delivery, including among them statues and bas-reliefs of children.

Beyond the stoa, you will come to the temple of Artemis with its

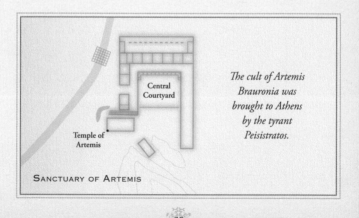

The cult of Artemis Brauronia was brought to Athens by the tyrant Peisistratos.

Central Courtyard

Temple of Artemis

SANCTUARY OF ARTEMIS

THE FIRST PRIESTESS

In the story that was immortalised by Euripides, the goddess Artemis demands the sacrifice of king Agamemnon's daughter, Iphigeneia, before the Greeks' becalmed ships may proceed to Troy. At the last minute the goddess snatches the girl away and takes her to Tauris on the Black Sea to be her priestess.

Years later, Iphigeneia is rescued by her brother, and they travel to Attica, taking the statue of Artemis with them. Instead of following her brother to Athens – where he will be tried for their mother's murder – Iphigeneia takes the statue to Artemis' temple in Brauron, and becomes its first priestess.

According to legend, Iphigeneia, daughter of Agamemnon, conqueror of Troy, was the first priestess at Brauron.

fine bronze doors and brazen cult image of the goddess. Beneath the temple is the sacred spring, into which pilgrims cast their offerings of vases, figurines, mirrors and even jewellery.

A cave between the temple and the acropolis is believed to be the tomb of Iphigeneia, the first priestess of the shrine (see box). Unfortunately, the roof of the cave collapsed recently, and it can no longer be entered. Other caves nearby hold the mortal remains of subsequent priestesses of Artemis.

RHAMNOUS

A fortified Attic deme, Rhamnous is 211 stadia northeast of Athens and 60 stadia north from the battle site of Marathon (see pp. 94–5).

The walled acropolis is built on a hill overlooking two small anchorages. The facilities of the town include a gymnasium and palaestra, a theatre, a public fountain house and a shrine to the cult-hero and god of healing, Amphiaraos. The town commands outstanding views of the Euboean Gulf and the island beyond.

Since the outbreak of the Spartan war, Rhamnous – one of the five Attic demes garrisoned by ephebes on their two-year military service – has become a vital point of import for Euboean grain.

SANCTUARIES OF THE GODDESSES

Rhamnous is famous for its ancient cult of the goddesses Nemesis and Themis (see boxes). The temple of Nemesis has stood on this site for over a century, but the original building was destroyed during the Persian invasion.

To reach the twin shrines, exit by the Marathon Gate from the acropolis and walk south for about 3.5 stadia. On your way you will pass many burials, both ancient and modern, topped with either simple earthen mounds or elaborate carved monuments.

Rhamnous overlooks the rocky coastline of northern Africa.

'SHE OF GOOD COUNSEL'

The older temple of Themis stands close by the sanctuary of Nemesis. The building is much smaller, measuring 35 pedes by 21 pedes. It is a joint dedication to the goddesses Themis and Nemesis, although the cult image within is of Themis. She is the daughter of Gaia, the Earth, and Uranus, the Sky, and embodies the natural order, law and custom. She is often paired with Nemesis, who brings swift retribution to those who ignore her divine sister's ordinances.

SHE WHO IS OWED HER DUE

Nemesis, one of the goddesses of Rhamnous, is the daughter of the titan Okeanos, the primeval ocean that girds the world, and the goddess of the night, Nyx. She is the personification of divine justice and retribution against those who succumb to arrogance or pride. She is honoured in Athens in the festival of the Nemeseia, which is meant to ward off the harm that the vengeful dead might do to the living.

TEMPLE OF NEMESIS

The new Doric temple, which is built on a broad platform with a 150-pedes retaining wall, was begun about 15 years ago and is still unfinished, its construction interrupted by the war. You will notice that the columns have not yet been fluted and that the spurs that protect the marble base blocks have yet to be removed.

In plan, it resembles the temples of Hephaistos in Athens (see p. 68) and of Poseidon in Sounion (see p. 87), which have led many to believe that they are the work of the same architect – although it is slightly smaller than both of these.

Although it has little in the way of external decoration, the temple houses the marvellous cult image of the goddess carved by either Pheidias or, some say, by his student Agorakritos.

The colossal statue stands 43 pedes high and was carved from a single block of Parian marble brought by the Persians to make their own victory trophy, but whose arrogance and blasphemy the goddess rightly punished. She is shown standing with an apple bough in her left hand and a bowl with motifs of Ethiopians in her right. Her crown consists of stags and small Nikai (victories).

The base of the statue depicts Helen brought by Nemesis to Leda, and heroes of the Trojan War, including Achilles.

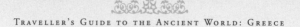

Battle Sites of the Persian Wars

The names of Salamis and Marathon echo gloriously in the annals of military history. On the plain of Marathon, the Athenian hoplites and their Plataian allies faced down the might of Darios' army 75 years ago; while ten years later, the allied and Athenian fleet overcame huge odds to defeat Darius' son Xerxes at Salamis.

MARATHON

The deme of Marathon is located on the northeastern coast of Attica. Its broad, marshy plain is isolated from the rest of Attica by Mount Pentelikon (see p. 11).

This plain is the site of the overwhelming victory that the Athenians and Plataians won over the Persian army of Darios 75

A visit to Marathon is interesting, but do not spend the night here – there are reports of the battlefield being haunted, and the clamour of battle still being audible after nightfall.

Battle of Marathon

The Persian army chose to land at Marathon because the area was one of the few in Attica suited to cavalry manoeuvres. The Athenians dispatched 10,000 hoplites and called for reinforcements from their Greek allies, but only the Plataians arrived in time.

The strategy of Miltiades', the Athenian commander, was to weaken his centre and reinforce his wings. At dawn he ordered his heavily armoured hoplites to run the exhausting 11 stadia towards the enemy lines.

As planned, the Athenian centre slowed, drawing the Persians in, and the wings closed in from the sides. The Persians panicked and retreated, and thousands were slaughtered before they could reach their ships.

Although outnumbered at Marathon, the Greek hoplites were better armed and trained than their enemies.

years ago (see box). The Athenians lost 192 men compared to Persian casualties of 6,400.

Visitors can see the mound that was erected over the communal grave of the fallen Athenians and another over that of their allies, the Plataians. A shrine to Herakles stands where the allies camped before the battle. After the victory, the Athenians set up a marble trophy on the northeast edge of the plain where most of the Persians died.

SALAMIS

Salamis is an island in the Saronic Gulf, west of Piraeus, which can be reached by ferry (fare: 1–2 obols). Although the island has never been an Attic deme, it became part of the Athenian state under Kleisthenes.

The island is sacred to Ajax the Great, hero of the Trojan War. After the naval victory of Salamis (see box) the Athenians set up a trophy on the coast overlooking the battle site.

BATTLE OF SALAMIS

A Greek fleet of some 374 triremes, 200 of which were Athenian, faced the might of the Persian navy of between 650 and 800 ships in the straits between the island of Salamis and the mainland. The Greeks were trapped, and the Persians expected an easy victory because of their overwhelming numbers.

The Greek fleet attacked at dawn but quickly retreated. Legend has it that a ghostly woman appeared wailing, 'How far will the Greeks retreat', spurring the Greek triremes to attack again.

The much larger Persian fleet could not manoeuvre in the narrow straits, and their ships rammed one another as much as the Greeks. At the height of the battle the Persian admiral was killed, and the Persian squadrons retreated in disarray, only to become entangled with the rest of the Persian fleet behind.

As the battle drew to a close, 200 Persians ships had been sunk or captured, and the second Persian invasion of Greece had been seriously compromised.

THE INTERIOR

THE MESOGEIA, THE INTERIOR OF ATTICA, IS DRY, FORESTED
AND MOUNTAINOUS, BUT IT DOES STILL PRODUCE WINE AND
OIL, AND IS SUITABLE FOR THE RAISING OF BOTH SHEEP AND
GOATS. THE MOUNTAIN RANGES PROVIDE THE CITY WITH
BUILDING STONE AND PARTICULARLY FINE WHITE AND VEINED
MARBLE. ALTHOUGH OFTEN CUT OFF FROM ATHENS BY THE
POVERTY OF THE ROADS, THE SUMMER FOREST FIRES AND
THE WINTER FLOODS, THE MESOGEIA IS WELL POPULATED,
WITH SEVERAL IMPORTANT DEMES, INCLUDING AKHARNAI,
IKARION AND DEKELEA.

MOUNT PARNES

Mount Parnes is a thickly forested mountain some 108 stadia north of Athens. It is still the haunt of the larger wild animals remaining in Attica: deer, boars, lions, bears and wolves. In the summer the upper slopes are used as pasture for sheep and goats, and the woods produce much of the charcoal needed for the braziers of the city. On the southern flank of the mountain is the fortified deme of Phyle, one of the five Attic forts garrisoned by the ephebes, Athenian youths doing their military service.

The town has a notable and ancient shrine to the goat-footed god Pan.

AKHARNAI

Located 65 stadia north of Athens and 43 stadia south of Mount Parnes, Akharnai is one of the most populous demes in Attica, with 72 representatives in the Boule. It is said to provide no fewer than 3,000 hoplites to the Athenian army.

The deme, which is famous for its hardy, simple charcoal burners, shepherds and farmers, was immortalised in Aristophanes' comedy *The Acharnians* (see pp. 148–9).

DEKELEA

Dekelea is located 120 stadia north of Athens, and controls the road from Boeotia to Athens. It is one of the main staging points for grain coming from Euboea.

The town has a sanctuary dedicated to Zeus and Leto, mother of the divine twins Apollo and Artemis. Although the town has many qualities, you would be wise to steer clear of its wine, which tastes like vinegar.

The forested and mountainous landscape of the Attic Mesogeia (the interior).

MOUNT PENTELIKON

Mount Pentelikon lies northeast of Athens and southwest of Marathon. The mountain is famed for the marble that has been used to build the temples of the Acropolis and many other famous buildings in Attica. Pentelikon's marble is particularly fine: flawless, unveined and of a warm white colour that glows with a golden hue in the sunlight.

IKARION

Ikarion is an Attic deme located 124 stadia north of Athens on the northern slopes of Mount Pentelikon. According to legend the deme was the first to adopt the worship of Dionysos, god of wine and vegetation, who has an important sanctuary in the town. Ikarion is also famous as the birthplace of Greek drama; and over 100 years ago, Thespis is said to have staged the first play featuring an actor playing with a chorus.

Alongside the temple of Dionysos is a stone theatre where plays are performed during the Rural Dionysia (see p. 107). Between the theatre and temple of Dionysos is the temple of Ikarian Apollo.

MOUNT HYMETTOS

Mount Hymettos is located west of Athens. Its forested slopes are renowned for their fragrant thyme and sweet, scented honey. The area also produces fine bluish-grey marble. The mountain has sanctuaries to Zeus and also to Apollo.

ENTERTAINMENT
ON A BUDGET

*A good day out in Athens and Attica is
synonymous with attending one of the 80 or so
festivals that take place throughout the year.
The Athenians celebrate the gods and heroes with a
bewildering array of activities: processions, sacrifices,
music, dance, poetry and, most famously, with
theatrical and athletic contests. Athens is also the
capital of the arts, with much to appreciate in
sculpture, painting, music, poetry and architecture. For
the bon-viveur, there are the pleasures
of good company, good wine and good fare –
though in Athens, the fare is more likely to be
intellectual than edible.*

FESTIVALS

 THE MAIN RELIGIOUS CELEBRATIONS OF THE ATTIC YEAR ARE THE LENAIA AND THE RURAL AND CITY DIONYSIA, WITH PROCESSIONS AND DRAMATIC CONTESTS HELD IN HONOUR OF DIONYSOS; THE GREATER MYSTERIES OF ELEUSIS, THE MYSTIC RITES OF DEMETER AND KORE; AND THE PANATHENAIA, THE FESTIVAL OF ATHENA, PATRON OF THE CITY, WHICH IS CELEBRATED WITH SPECIAL MAGNIFICENCE EVERY FOURTH YEAR.

HEKATOMBAION
(JUNE/JULY)

The Athenian year begins on the new moon after the summer solstice. On the 28th the procession of the Panathenaia (see pp. 102–3) is held to honour Athena. Other festivals include the Aphrodisia of Aphrodite Pandemos, on the 4th, and the Synoikia, on the 15th and 16th, which celebrates the unification of Attica.

METAGEITNION
(JULY/AUGUST)

The Eleusinia, from the 15th to the 18th, is a series of athletic contests held in Eleusis at which the prizes consist of measures of grain.

BOEDROMION
(AUGUST/SEPTEMBER)

The month of the Greater Eleusinian Mysteries, held on the 15th to 21st (see p. 84–5) witnesses nine days of celebration at Athens and Eleusis.

PYANEPSION
(SEPTEMBER/OCTOBER)

The highlight of the month is the all-female festival of the Thesmophoria, the 11th to the 13th, in which women freed from their usual obligations sleep in makeshift camps around the sanctuaries of Demeter. Held on the 7th is the Pyanepsia, the festival of Apollo during which boys go from house to house asking for gifts of food in exchange for blessings.

MAIMAKTERION
(OCTOBER/NOVEMBER)

The month when the cold weather begins is marked by sacrifices to Zeus and a procession, the Pompaia (in the last third of the month), dedicated to him.

POSEIDEION
(NOVEMBER/DECEMBER)

The dramatic contests and merry processions of the Rural Dionysia (see p. 107) are held all over Attica during the second half of Poseideion. On the 26th, women dance around a giant phallos in honour of Dionysos and Demeter during the Haloa.

GAMELION
(DECEMBER/JANUARY)

The Lenaia, held from the 12th to the 15th, another festival in honour of Dionysos, is one of three that feature dramatic contests in Athens. Because it is held in winter, it is easier to get seats at the Lenaia than at the City Dionysia (see p. 107). The Gamelia, on the 26th, celebrates the marriage of Zeus and Hera.

ANTHESTERION
(JANUARY/FEBRUARY)

The depth of winter is a suitable time for the Anthesteria, for this is the festival of the dead. It is held from the 11th to the 13th, and on the last day of the festival, the ghosts are banished with loud cries of 'Away with you! It's no longer Anthesteria!'

ELAPHEBOLION
(FEBRUARY/MARCH)

Along with the processions of the City Dionysia, held from the 9th to the 13th (see p. 107), the festival features the most important dramatic contests in Greece. Also celebrated are festivals to Artemis on the 6th, Asklepios on the 8th or 9th and Zeus Pandion on the 14th or 17th.

MOUNYCHION
(MARCH/APRIL)

The festival of Artemis Mounychia, on the 6th or 16th, is celebrated all over Attica, but especially magnificently at her shrine in Piraeus (see p. 81).

THARGELION
(APRIL/MAY)

The month is named for the Thargelia, held on the 6th and 7th, a festival of Apollo and Artemis during which a man and a woman are chosen as *pharmakoi* (scapegoats) and driven from the city. The last week of the month sees the Plynteria, the ritual washing of the statue of Athena Polias (see p. 53).

SKIRAPHORION
(MAY/JUNE)

The year closes with the festival of Arrhephoria on 3 Skiraphorion (see p. 55); the Skiraphoria on the 12th, a women's fertility festival; and the Bouphonia, or ox-killing festival (see p. 52). The last day of the old year is marked by the sacrifice of Zeus Soter and Athena Soteira ('Saviour') to ensure good fortune for the coming year.

PANATHENAIA

The Panathenaia (the All-Athens Festival) was instituted by Kekrops, the first king of Athens, after the Athenians had chosen Athena over Poseidon to be the city's patron.

The festival procession, or *pompe*, to the Altar of Athena on the Acropolis is held every year on Hekatombion 28, but is celebrated with special magnificence every fourth year, when the event is known as the Greater Panathenaia.

All freeborn residents of the city, citizens and metics, may take part, but only Athenian citizens are allowed to pass through the Propylaia and witness the ceremonies on the Acropolis. In addition to the pompe, sacrifice and ritual feasting, the Greater Panathenaia includes a number of artistic contests and athletics competitions.

LESSER PANATHENAIA

In the year of a Lesser Panathenaia, the procession begins at the Dipylon Gate in the Kerameikos and makes its way along the Panathenaic Way through the Agora to the Acropolis.

Sacrifices are offered on the hill of the Areopagos and on the altar of the temple of Athena Nike. The procession then crosses the Propylaia onto the rock proper, and proceeds to the Erechtheion, where the peplos woven by the women of Athens and the Arrhephoroi (see p. 55) is presented to the statue of Athena Polias.

The final act of the festival is the sacrifice of a bull on the open-air altar of Athena that stands between the Erechtheion and the Parthenon, followed by a ritual feast.

The procession assembles at dawn at the Dipylon Gate. In the

The procession of the Panathenaia making its way along the Panathenaic Way.

WHAT TO EXPECT

POMPE OF THE GREAT PANATHENAIA

A century and a half ago, the tyrant Peisistratos (see p. 144) instituted an especially splendid celebration of the festival to be held every four years; this has become known as the Greater Panathenaia.

The festival is so popular with non-Athenians that it ranks alongside the Mysteries of Eleusis and the Olympic Games as a great pan-Hellenic celebration. If you cannot attend the festival itself, then you can get an idea of its sheer scale and magnificence by studying the inner Ionic frieze of the Parthenon (see p. 47), which shows the pompe of the Greater Panathenaia in detail.

lead you will see the *kanephoroi*, the basket-carriers, who carry the ritual and sacrificial paraphernalia. They are followed by the *hydriaphoroi*, water-jar carriers, and the *skaphephoroi*, who bear the trays of honeycombs and cakes used to entice the sacrificial animals to the altar. Next come the elders, musicians playing the kithara and aulos, the Archon Basileos and his officials, and the maidens and Arrephoroi carrying the new peplos for Athena Polias. A second, sail-sized peplos is displayed from the mast of a float in the shape of a boat. Behind this come the sacrificial victims for the hundred-ox sacrifice, the Hekatombion, and their attendants. The

procession closes with ten rows of six horsemen from the ten phylai and the charioteers who will take part in the apobates contest during the Panathenaic Games.

Ikria, or spectator stands, are erected along the route in the Agora, but as the seats are reserved for officials, ephebes and citizens, you will be unlikely to obtain one unless you are well connected.

To get a good view of the procession, your best bet is to get up well before sunrise, and stand where the Panathenaic Way enters or leaves the Agora.

A hydriaphoroi, or water-jar carrier, in the procession of the Panathenaia.

SPORTS EVENTS

THE WHOLE OF GREECE IS FAMOUS FOR ITS GAMES, MOST NOTABLY THOSE HELD EVERY FOUR YEARS AT THE SANCTUARY OF OLYMPIA, BUT THERE ARE PLENTY OF SPORTING SPECTACLES TO BEEN SEEN IN ATHENS ITSELF. THE MOST IMPRESSIVE OF THESE IS THE PANATHENAIC GAMES THAT IS HELD EVERY FOUR YEARS DURING THE GREATER PANATHENAIA.

PANATHENAIC GAMES

The games are held every four years as part of the Greater Panathenaia, which lasts several days longer than the smaller annual festival. Although the games are the most important in Attica and attract competitors from all over the Greek world, they do not rank with the pan-Hellenic games held at Olympia, Delphi or Corinth.

Naked hoplites take part in the armoured race wearing greaves and a helmet, and carrying a shield.

The games are divided into two: a section open to all Greek athletes, and one limited to Athenians only, which is staged as a competition between teams drawn from the ten phyllai. In addition to the athletic events, the games also include contests for the best rhapsodic recitation of Homer's *Odyssey* and *Iliad*, and for performances on the *aulos* (flute), the *diaulos* (double flute) and the *kithara* (lyre), all of which are held in the Odeion next to the theatre of Dionysos.

TAKING PART

The section of the games that is open to all comers includes all the usual events held at a major Greek sporting meet such as foot races, wrestling, pankration, pentathlon (stadion race, wrestling, long jump, javelin and discus throw) and equestrian events.

As is usual, the athletes compete naked, with their bodies oiled and sprinkled with sand. The dromos (racetrack) on the Agora is one stadion long by 124 pedes wide,

FOR THE ATHENIANS ONLY

On the fifth and final day of the festival games, the events reserved for the ten Athenian phyllai take place. These include both day-time and night-time events. Many of the events held on the Agora during the day have a martial flavour, which indicates their origins as a form of military training. There are mock infantry and cavalry battles; a competition of throwing javelins from horseback; the *apobates*, in which men in full armour leap on and off racing chariots; and the *pyrriche*, a military dance performed to the musical accompaniment of the diaulos.

Another event that is unique to the Panathenaic Games is the Euandria, a male beauty and strength contest in which only Athenian athletes are allowed to take part.

The night-time events consist of two torch relay races, one from Piraeus to the Acropolis, a distance of some 38 stadia, and one from the altar of Prometheus in the Akademeia, along the Panathenaic Way, through the Agora, to the Altar of Athena on the Acropolis, over a distance of 13.5 stadia. The winning team is rewarded with the prize of 100 drachmai.

from the start next to the altar of the Twelve Gods to the finish line in front of the South Stoa.

There are three main running events: the one-stadion sprint, the middle-distance *hippios*, over five stadia, and the long-distance foot race over 22 stadia. Each has four heats followed by a final. There are several other foot races, including the *hoplitodromos*, or armour race, in which competitors wear a helmet and greaves and carry a shield.

The pentathlon events are the discus, javelin, long jump, the one-stadion race and wrestling.

The winners are rewarded with amphorae of the olive oil pressed from the fruit of the 12 sacred *moriai* (olive trees) in the grove of Athena in the Akademeia.

On the fourth day of the festival, the equestrian events are held in a suitably open location outside the city walls. These consist of horse and chariot races, for two- and four-horse chariots. The most prestigious (and dangerous) event of the games is the two-horse chariot race, whose winner is awarded no less than 140 amphorae of oil.

THEATRE

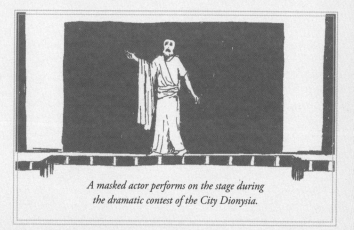

THE FIRST PROFESSIONAL 'ACTOR', IT IS SAID, WAS THESPIS OF IKARION. HE WAS THE LEADER OF A DITHYRAMBIC CHORUS, A GROUP OF 50 MEN AND BOYS WHO COMPETE IN SINGING HYMNS TO DIONYSOS DURING THE GOD'S FESTIVALS. SOMETIME DURING THE MIDDLE OF THE LAST CENTURY, HE HIT UPON THE IDEA OF 'ACTING' THE PARTS OF THE CHARACTERS IN THE HYMNS BY WEARING DIFFERENT MASKS AND ENGAGING IN DIALOGUES WITH THE CHORUS, ALSO COSTUMED AND MASKED. THE NEW STYLE WAS DUBBED 'TRAGEDY', AND IT PROVED SO POPULAR THAT A COMPETITION TO FIND THE BEST TRAGIC PLAY WAS SOON INSTITUTED IN ATHENS.

This was followed half a century later by a competition for the best comedy. Over the years, further actors were added, and today three actors and a chorus of 12 to 15 perform the plays.

There are three festivals in Attica in which the dramatic arts play a major role: the Lenaia, and the Rural and City Dionysia. Three tragic playwrights compete in the most prestigious of the three,

A masked actor performs on the stage during the dramatic contest of the City Dionysia.

the City Dionysia. The plays are produced by *choregoi*, wealthy citizens who pay for all expenses, such as hiring the theatre and actors and buying costumes and scenery. The victorious choregos is allowed to erect a tripod as a victory monument on the Street of the Tripods in Athens.

CITY DIONYSIA

The City Dionysia is in the charge of the Eponymous Archon, who organises the celebrations, selects the playwrights who will compete in the dramatic contests and appoints the choregoi who will pay for the productions.

On its first day, citizens, metics and soldiers march in a pompe, or procession, carrying a wooden statue of Dionysos Eleutherios and wood and bronze phalloi to the theatre of Dionysos on the south slope of the Acropolis. After the pompe, the choruses compete in the dithyrambic contests. The first day ends with the sacrifice of a bull, ritual feasting and general drunken revelry.

The following day, the *proagon*, the pre-contest introduction of the plays, is held in the Odeion.

The next three days are devoted to the main event of the festival, the performance of nine tragedies and three satyr plays.

On the sixth day, playwrights compete for the prize of best comedy. The judges announce the winners of the dramatic contests on the final day of the festival, and the day ends with a pompe and another night of drunken revelry.

LENAIA

The festival of Lenaia takes place in Athens in the winter month of Gamelion. As in the City Dionysia, the celebrations begin with a pompe and sacrifice in honour of Dionysos. In contrast to the latter festival, however, comedy is the main dramatic form celebrated, and there are no dithyrambic contests. At the time of writing, because of the ongoing Spartan war, only three comedies are performed instead of the usual five.

RURAL DIONYSIA

There is a second Dionysia, the Rural Dionysia, celebrated all over Attica during the winter month of Poseideion. Each deme celebrates the festival on different days, so it is possible to attend several of the events. The main draw is the pompe, followed by singing and dancing contests and the performance of 'dithyrambic choruses', competitions for the recital of short poems.

The larger demes such as Piraeus, Thorikos and Ikarion, have their own theatres and stage dramatic contests of the plays that have been performed at the previous year's City Dionysia.

The theatre of Dionysos filling up in the early hours of the first day of the Lenaia.

The three tragedies and one satyr play written by each of the competing playwrights are played on successive days, with interludes of poetry, dance and choral performances. As the day's performance lasts seven to eight hours, you will find food and drink are on sale in the theatre.

GOING TO THE THEATRE

Going to the theatre is not expensive. A day's attendance costs two obols, which is within the reach of most Athenians, and for those who cannot afford even this small sum, there is the public 'seeing fund'.

Getting a token for a seat, though, is another matter. Although the theatre of Dionysos can seat several thousand, performances are generally oversubscribed. The admission tokens are not sold to the public but allocated to VIPs, officials, ephebes and then the general citizenry. Out-of-towners have to count on the generosity of locals, who may be persuaded to part with their tokens, or approach their *proxenos* (see p. 136) to see if he can obtain a seat for them. If you cannot get seats, the only alternative is to watch from the rocky slope above the theatre.

TRAGEDY AND COMEDY

The festivals feature two genres: tragedy and comedy. Tragedies are based on well-known stories involving gods and men. The *Oresteia*, written a little over 40 years ago by Aeskhylos, is considered by many to be the finest tragic trilogy ever written. Its themes of betrayal and retribution, and the powerlessness of humans in front of fate, are timeless.

Comedies, on the other hand, deal with topical subjects that involve ordinary folk, and are often political in tone. At present, comedies critical of the war with Sparta are much in vogue.

Both tragedies and comedies are performed by professional troupes consisting of three male actors and an all-male chorus. The permanent wooden skene behind the orchestra acts as a general backdrop, although painted scenery is also sometimes used. The gods usually deliver their lines from the upper part of the *skene*, and in recent years a *mechane* – a type of crane – has been introduced to lift and lower actors as if in flight.

GREAT PLAYWRIGHTS

Although every Athenian will have their own favourite playwright – and indeed these are the subject of much debate – some are universally revered. Among these acclaimed few are Aeskhylos, Sophokles and Euripides – three playwrights whose works have revolutionised the world of the stage.

Recognised as the father of tragedy, Aeskhylos increased the number of characters in his plays, allowing for greater dramatic conflict between them. One of his most celebrated plays, *The Persians*, deals with the defeat of the Persians under Xerxes at the battle of Plataia eleven years after the battle of Marathon, where the playwright himself had fought.

Aeskhylos

For close on half a century, Sophokles has been the most celebrated playwright of the City Dionysia. He has competed in more than 30 dramatic contests, winning 24 and never being placed any lower than second. His most famous tragic trilogy deals with the life of King Oedipus.

Euripides brings to the stage a new type of

Sophokles

drama that mixes the tragic and comic. His plays, while still putting on stage great epic tales of gods and men, such as the Trojan War, examine the individual psychology of the characters rather than social issues or lofty philosophical themes. His innovations are not to everyone's tastes, however, and his plays have not been crowned with success in competition.

He remains, though, without doubt the greatest comedic talent of the age. Many of his plays are political and poke fun at the leaders of the city and their conduct of the Spartan war. He has been prosecuted several times for defaming Athens in front of the foreigners who flock to see his plays, but such is his popularity that he has yet to be convicted.

Euripides

APPRECIATING THE ARTS

THE DEMES OF ATTICA ARE VERITABLE TREASURIES OF THE VISUAL ARTS. WHETHER YOU ARE INTERESTED IN THE FIELD OF SCULPTURE, PAINTING OR ARCHITECTURE, YOU CAN BE SURE TO FIND THE BEST OF GREECE IN THE REGION. UNRIVALLED FOR ARCHITECTURE SINCE THE TIME OF PERIKLES, THE PUBLIC BUILDINGS AND TEMPLES OF ATHENS ALSO HOUSE OUTSTANDING COLLECTIONS OF SCULPTURE AND PAINTING THAT YOU CAN ADMIRE FREE OF CHARGE.

The Greeks divide the arts into two: that which is permanent, such as sculpture, painting and architecture, which is known as *tekne*; and that which is temporary, such as the work of musicians, dramatists and poets, which is termed *sophia*.

There has been a great evolution in the arts in the past few centuries. In ancient times, the arts – both tekne and sophia – were epic and heroic, depicting worlds beyond the everyday, but over the course of the past century these loftier, more severe styles have given way to more approachable and naturalistic representations of humanity. To apply the philosopher Heraklitos' description of modern sculpture to all art forms: 'everything flows'.

SCULPTURE

In ancient times, the bulk of statuary to be found in Attica was images of the gods, or kouroi and

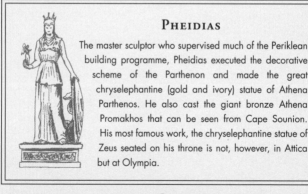

PHEIDIAS

The master sculptor who supervised much of the Periklean building programme, Pheidias executed the decorative scheme of the Parthenon and made the great chryselephantine (gold and ivory) statue of Athena Parthenos. He also cast the giant bronze Athena Promakhos that can be seen from Cape Sounion. His most famous work, the chryselephantine statue of Zeus seated on his throne is not, however, in Attica but at Olympia.

korai (see p. 51), the stiffly posed and idealised statues of men and women that were offered to the gods and used as grave markers. The invading Persians smashed and burned many of these early works, but a few did survive, and they stand in marked contrast to modern sculpture.

Since the establishment of the democracy at the beginning of the century, the role and form of sculpture has changed. Now, in addition to depicting the gods, sculptors create more naturalistic images of men and women engaged in real pursuits. It is said that the original statue of the tyrannicides Harmodios and Aristogeiton that stood in the Agora (see p. 69) was the first public monument erected to real people. Another example is the Ionic frieze of the Parthenon, which depicts the participants of the Greater Panathenaic pompe.

PAINTING

The highest form of the painter's art is painting on sanides, or wooden panels. These depict a mixture of historical and religious subjects, such as famous Greek and Athenian victories and the war of the giants against the gods, as well as portraits of famous men and scenes of daily life. You will find collections of sanides exhibited in the stoas of the Agora and in the temples of the Acropolis.

POLYGNOTOS

One of the greatest painters of the mid-century, Polygnotos was born on the island of Thasos but was granted Athenian citizenship by the Ekklesia. His paintings are on display in the Stoa Poikile (see pp. 64–5), which takes its name from his sanides of *The Fall of Troy* and *The Marriage of the Daughters of Leukippos*, and in the Pinakotheke of the Propylaia (see p. 42). An accomplished draftsman, he used a restricted palette of colours and simple compositions of great nobility and power.

The red figure wares of Athens are a notable part of its artistic culture.

*The Doric order metopes and triglyphs
from the Parthenon.*

ARCHITECTURE

Even in Mycenaean times, the Athenians built great stone palaces, tombs and temples, and their remains can still be seen all over Athens and Attica. The buildings of the subsequent 'Dark Ages', however, were made of perishable materials and have not survived.

When the city grew wealthy and more populous around three and a half centuries ago, the Athenians began to build once more in stone. Attica is blessed with plentiful, high-quality dark limestone from Eleusis and the finest, lustrous marbles from Mount Hymettos and Mount Pentelikon.

Although the private dwellings of Attica are seldom grand, since the time of Peisistratos her temples and civic buildings have been made of the finest materials and ornamented with extensive sculptural decoration.

The traditional floor plan of a temple is rectangular, with a *proanos*, or front porch, *naos*, or cella, where the cult statue and votive offerings are housed, and opisthodomos, or rear porch. There is no hard-and-fast rule as to the shape of a temple, however, as can be seen in the unusual layout of the Erechtheion (see pp. 48–51), with its double cella and the proanos to the side of the building.

Most public buildings are stoas: long rectangular structures with a colonnade at the front and rooms within. The grandest in Athens is the Stoa of Zeus Eleutherios (see p. 65), on the northwest side of the Agora. While temples can be made entirely of stone and marble, lesser buildings are usually made of brick with stone façades and decorative elements.

One of the most unusual buildings in Athens is the Tholos (see pp. 66–7), the circular chamber of the Prytaneion, crowned with a conical roof, and reminiscent of a more ancient style of building.

ORDERS

There are two architectural orders used in Athens: the severe Doric, and the lighter, more decorative Ionic (see p. 45). Many buildings incorporate both; for example, the predominantly Doric Parthenon has a continuous Ionic frieze and Ionic columns in the interior. The Propylaia and several of the Agora stoas have Doric façades with internal Ionic columns. The Erechtheion, on the other hand, has no Doric elements, probably because its irregular shape meant that a Doric scheme would look too heavy and ungainly.

The issue of cost also enters into play when choosing the order of a building, because of the greater quantities of stone needed for the more massive Doric columns, friezes and pediments.

BUILDING DECORATION

Private houses have little or no decoration beyond whitewashed or painted internal walls. Only the very wealthiest can afford frescoes, and these are rare in Atttica, where this kind of private ostentation is frowned upon.

In their public buildings, however, and in particular in their dedications to the gods, the Athenians show no such restraint, and some might even say that some of the decoration of their temples verges on the garish. Externally, the pediments and friezes are painted in vivid colours against a dark background. This makes the scenes, which can be 30 pedes from the ground, much easier to see.

Internally, the decorations may also be quite lavish, with elaborate colonnades and painted coffered ceilings, such as those of the Propylaia and the temple of Hephaistos (see p. 68).

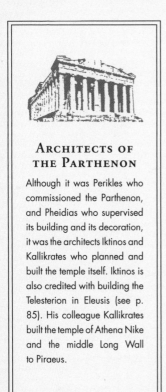

ARCHITECTS OF THE PARTHENON

Although it was Perikles who commissioned the Parthenon, and Pheidias who supervised its building and its decoration, it was the architects Iktinos and Kallikrates who planned and built the temple itself. Iktinos is also credited with building the Telesterion in Eleusis (see p. 85). His colleague Kallikrates built the temple of Athena Nike and the middle Long Wall to Piraeus.

SYMPOSIA

THE SYMPOSION, OR SYMPOSIUM, IS AN ARTISTIC AND
INTELLECTUAL GATHERING OF INFLUENTIAL CITIZENS, ARTISTS
AND PHILOSOPHERS, USUALLY ALL MALE, THOUGH SEVERAL
EXCEPTIONAL FEMALE GUESTS MAY BE PRESENT ALONG WITH
THE HIRED FLUTE GIRLS AND SERVING SLAVES. ALTHOUGH
THE CONVERSATION AT THE BEGINNING OF THE EVENING MAY
BE ELEVATED AND REFINED, AS THE GUESTS IMBIBE GREATER
AND GREATER QUANTITIES OF WINE, THE EVENT BECOMES
EVER MORE RIOTOUS AND BAWDIER, AND IT USUALLY ENDS IN
THE MOST LICENTIOUS BEHAVIOUR.

Unless you are extremely fortunate – in other words unless you are a wealthy foreign visitor, or a very handsome young man, or otherwise well connected in the city – it is unlikely that you will be invited to a symposion.

Symposia are often held in the official dining rooms of temples and public buildings, but if you want to see the event at its most typical, you will have to attend one in the *andron* (men's quarters) of a private house.

WHAT TO EXPECT

PARTY OR ORGY?

Although some symposia can be extremely elevated and restrained affairs, at which matters of state and philosophical themes are discussed, they can also be thinly disguised orgies in which fellow guests, slave boys and flute girls are all fair game. As we shall see overleaf, the Athenians, like most Greeks, have little compunction about public nudity (at least on the part of men) and sexual conduct, and are little concerned with accusations of immorality.

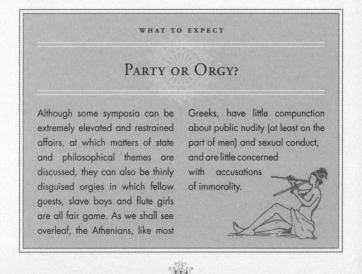

The host of the symposion, the *symposiarch*, acts as the master of ceremonies. He decides how much water to add to the wine, and thereby how quickly his fellow symposiasts will become drunk. He sets the tone for the proceedings, which could be intellectual and elevated, or bawdy and licentious from the start.

Symposia are given for a variety of reasons such as to celebrate a victory in an athletic or dramatic contest or to introduce a young man into Athenian high society. The guests, as a rule, are all male, but notable women such as *hetaira* (high-class courtesans) attend symposia and discuss matters of state and philosophy with the men. Even when women guests are not present, female company is provided by 'flute girls', who, in addition to providing the musical accompaniments to songs and poems on the aulos, are also paid prostitutes.

PARTY GAMES

Once the guests have assembled, the symposiarch offers a libation to the gods, and to Dionysos, god of wine, in particular. The guests recline singly or in pairs on couches arranged around the walls of the andron; though youths do not recline, but sit.

Naked boy slaves chosen for their looks mix the wine with water in the large central *krater* (mixing bowl) and serve it to each guest in large, shallow cup known as a *kylix*, serve food – though the fare, as ever, is not always luxurious, consisting of bread and opson (see p. 129), and figs and sweet cakes for dessert.

The symposiarch suggests the topic of conversation and invites contributions from the guests; or, if he has a more diverting evening planned, he may opt for party games instead. One of the most popular is *kottabos*, in which players swish the dregs of their kylixes at a target on a small bronze statuette. Other games include singing and drinking contests, the aim of which is to get the guests as drunk as possible.

Guests relaxing during a symposion.

SEX AND THE
BROTHELS OF ATHENS

REFLECTING THE LOCAL VIEW OF SEX, AN ATHENIAN PHILOSOPHER ONCE SAID: 'WE HAVE COURTESANS FOR PLEASURE, CONCUBINES TO PROVIDE FOR OUR DAILY NEEDS, AND OUR SPOUSES TO GIVE US LEGITIMATE CHILDREN AND TO BE THE FAITHFUL GUARDIANS OF OUR HOMES.' SEX IS NOT LIMITED TO HETEROSEXUAL CONDUCT IN ATHENS, AND PEDERASTIC RELATIONSHIPS BETWEEN MEN AND BOYS HAVE AN IMPORTANT ROLE TO PLAY IN SOCIAL LIFE, EDUCATION AND MILITARY TRAINING.

Like other patriarchal societies, Athens sets different standards of behaviour for men and women, youths and adults, and freeborn citizens and slaves. Although a father may be content for his adolescent son to spend his days at the gymnasium naked, where he will be courted by older boys and men, he locks his daughter in the gynakeion and expects her to be veiled in public, and to be a virgin until her wedding night.

Similarly, while adult men have a great deal of latitude in terms of their behaviour, taking both male and female lovers and visiting brothels, their wives are expected to be faithful and chaste. If a husband catches his wife in the arms of another, he is entitled to kill her without fear of legal consequences.

The Greeks are also famous for their friendships between men,

but though it is quite acceptable for boys and youths who have not reached maturity (which is defined as being able to grow a beard) to be courted by older men, it would be considered strange if two adult men entered into a permanent relationship. Sex with slaves is

The great lawgiver Solon was the first to create state brothels.

WHAT TO EXPECT

PROSTITUTION

Prostitution is common in Attica, and it is said that the great reformer Solon (see p. 144) created the first state *porneia*, or brothels, so that citizens would never be lacking in sexual comforts. All the larger urban demes have both male and female brothels; in Athens you will find them near the city gates, in particular the Dipylon and Sacred Gates in the Kerameikos, and in Piraeus they are situated near the city gates and the Kantharos harbour.

There are several ranks of prostitutes. The lowest grade is that of the *pornai*: foreign slaves who work in brothels, and whose services can be purchased for a few obols. Next come the independent prostitutes: freeborn women who sell their services on a part-time basis. They are often employed as flute girls at symposia, for which they are paid two drachmas, the same as a working man's daily wage. The highest grade is that of the *hetairai*, who are beautiful, highly educated courtesans and charge up to 10,000 drachmas for one night.

permissible, and in their case no restrictions apply as to age and sex, as they are considered to be 'non-persons'.

SAME-SEX RELATIONS

Pederasty, or friendship between men and youths, is institutionalised in the Greek world. The *erastes*, the adult male lover, pursues the *eromenos*, the adolescent, with declarations of love and devotion, promising to mentor him in the ways of life. In its idealised form, carnal love may not figure in the relationship, but in reality, sex between men and boys is fairly common in a culture where men and women are segregated, and men do not marry on average until the age of 30.

Pederasty is synonymous with the culture of gymnasia, where athletes exercise naked, and where older men tutor youths in sport and the martial arts. Similar relationships between women and adolescent girls are hinted at in literature, but given the closed nature of the gynakeion, it is difficult to confirm or deny the existence of such a custom.

PRACTICAL
CONSIDERATIONS

*This section provides a visitor with all the practical
information he or she might need for a stay in Athens
and Attica. Travellers to the region should not expect a
problem-free trip. Quite apart from the perils of the
present war with Sparta, there are the usual dangers of
travelling by land and sea, and the difficulty in finding
suitable accommodation, especially at festival time
(which is most of the time in Athens). Furthermore, as
a foreigner, your civil rights are limited should you get
into trouble during your stay. On the plus side, you will
find the Athenians a lively, welcoming people, who love
novelty, and who – as long as their superiority is
acknowledged – are tolerant of non-Attic Greeks
and barbarians alike.*

How to Get There

THE CITIES OF THE GREEK WORLD HUG THE SHORES OF THE MIDDLE SEA LIKE FROGS SITTING AROUND A POND. HENCE, THE MOST COMMON FORM OF LONG-DISTANCE TRANSPORT IS BY SEA. ATTICA IS BLESSED WITH MANY FINE ANCHORAGES, AND TRADING VESSELS REGULARLY SAIL FROM HER PORTS TO THE FOUR CORNERS OF THE KNOWN WORLD. TRAVELLING OVERLAND IS ALSO AN OPTION, BUT A MORE ARDUOUS AND DANGEROUS ONE, BECAUSE OF THE CONDITION OF THE ROADS AND THE LAWLESSNESS OF RURAL AREAS.

ARRIVING BY SEA

Most travellers in the Greek world travel by ship, and even visitors from other parts of Attica often prefer to come to Athens by sea rather than overland. This is easy to explain when you understand the state of the roads, which we shall examine below.

The seaborne traveller is spared the physical exertion of those who must travel on land, but the sea has its own dangers: storms and shipwreck, pirates and enemy ships. Since the Athenian victories over the Persian and Spartan fleets, however, attacks in Attic waters are unlikely. Mariners do not put to sea in winter when the danger of storms is too great, so the sailing season starts in the spring, continuing until the end of fall.

The large, heavy and relatively slow merchantmen, which are known as 'round ships', ply the routes between Asian Ionia, the Levant, the Aegean Islands and Magna Graecia, calling at all the major ports of the Middle Sea. Most will take passengers to increase the

The most comfortable way to get to Attica is by sea.

profitability of the voyage. Do not expect many creature comforts on board. There is usually a small deckhouse and a few cabins, but these will most likely be taken by the captain and crew and the wealthiest passengers. You will have to bring your own food and wine, and either you or your slave will have to take your turn cooking meals in the ship's galley.

Your first act, when arriving safely at Piraeus (see pp. 78–81) or Sounion (see pp. 86–7), should be to go straight to the temple of Poseidon and make an offering of thanks for your safe arrival.

ARRIVING BY LAND

Attica is a peninsula cut off from the rest of Greece by mountain ranges. An overland trip not only takes you through difficult terrain, it also means crossing the territory of states currently hostile to Athens: Corinth to the west and Boeotia to the northwest. Your best option is to come during one of the sacred truces (see box).

Dismal and dangerous roads await the overland traveller.

Broad, rutted roads suitable for wheeled vehicles are rare in Greece, but there are three in Attica, all leading to Athens: from Piraeus, Eleusis and from Mount Pentelikon. Most other roads are narrow and sometimes too steep to allow the passage of carts, so most people travel on foot with their slaves and perhaps with a mule or donkey to carry the baggage.

Unless you are travelling on one of the major highways, you will find few inns and will have to carry your own food. Bandits haunt the less populous areas, so you would be well advised to travel in a group or hire bodyguards for the duration of your trip.

SACRED TRUCES

Sacred truces are announced to coincide with important pan-Hellenic festivals so as to enable pilgrims to attend without fear of being caught up in hostilities. The most famous of these is the month-long truce for the Olympic Games. In Attica, a truce is called every year for the celebration of the Greater Mysteries of Eleusis.

ACCOMMODATION

FINDING SUITABLE ACCOMMODATION IN ATHENS AND ATTICA IS NO EASY TASK. MERCHANTS STAY WITH THEIR BUSINESS CONTACTS, AND THOSE WITH CONNECTIONS IN THE CITY — ESPECIALLY THE WELL-TO-DO — WITH FRIENDS OR RELATIVES. HOWEVER, FOR THE ORDINARY VISITOR THE CHOICE IS BETWEEN INNS, TEMPLE LODGINGS OR SLEEPING IN PUBLIC BUILDINGS. AN ALTERNATIVE FOR LONGER STAYS IS TO RENT A ROOM IN A PRIVATE HOUSE.

A visitor to Athens is well advised to arrive by day. Finding your way in the snaking lanes of the city in darkness, with no lights or street signs to guide you, would be both foolish and dangerous; not least because of the risk of being mugged, or more humiliatingly doused in excrement from someone emptying a chamber pot. Even in daylight, finding your way can be a challenge, as directions tend to be based around local landmarks, which you should take every care to familiarise yourself with.

Large public inns are to be found in the major towns and along the main highways.

PRIVATE HOSPITALITY

If you are fortunate to have a wealthy relative or business associate, you will no doubt be invited to stay in his *xenon* (guestroom). Unless you are close friends or kin, you will be invited to his table on the evening of your arrival, but thereafter will have to make your own eating arrangements.

PANDOKEION

If you have no connections in Attica, you will have to seek lodging in a *pandokeion* (place for receiving all-comers) or a public inn. You can find these on major highways and in the larger towns, especially in Athens and the busier ports. Be warned: these establishments have the reputation of being dirty, cramped and the haunts of both bedbugs and women of easy virtue. As a rule, they are run by women, though 'gorgon' or 'harpy' is locally thought to be a more appropriate term.

A chamber pot is the best that you can expect at an inn.

A typical inn is a two-storey building within a walled courtyard. The shared rooms have sleeping pallets but no other furniture or bedclothes. You can request a brazier in the winter months, but there is no guarantee that you will get one.

Do not expect bathing and toilet facilities other than the most basic chamber pot. Town inns do not provide meals (see pp. 128–9), so you will have make your own arrangements.

In the country, where there are no markets or taverns, you should agree a price for each item that you require – room, food, stabling, wine and so on – as there is no set price for bed and board together.

TEMPLES

Several of the larger shrines in Attica, such as Brauron and Eleusis, operate their own inns for pilgrims, and these will be of slightly better quality than private establishments. However, while these may be cleaner, more salubrious and better run, they do not offer any better facilities.

PUBLIC BUILDINGS

For those who lack the funds to stay even in an inn, there is the shelter of public buildings, such as stoas and the porches and colonnades of temples. However, this is an option fraught with danger because of the criminals, ruffians and drunkards who haunt the streets at night.

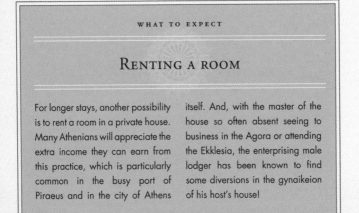

WHAT TO EXPECT

RENTING A ROOM

For longer stays, another possibility is to rent a room in a private house. Many Athenians will appreciate the extra income they can earn from this practice, which is particularly common in the busy port of Piraeus and in the city of Athens itself. And, with the master of the house so often absent seeing to business in the Agora or attending the Ekklesia, the enterprising male lodger has been known to find some diversions in the gynaikeion of his host's house!

MANNERS AND CUSTOMS

UNLIKE THE MILITARY SPARTANS, WHO ARE RAISED WITH THEIR PEERS IN A BARRACKS, THE ATHENIANS HOLD THE FAMILY TO BE THE MOST IMPORTANT SOCIAL INSTITUTION. ATHENIANS LIVE IN MULTI-GENERATIONAL HOUSEHOLDS, WITH GREAT HONOUR ACCORDED TO THE ELDERS AND THE FATHER OF THE HOUSE, WHOSE WORD IS LAW. MARRIAGES, CHILD-NAMINGS AND FUNERALS ARE THE MOST IMPORTANT CELEBRATIONS FOR A FAMILY AND ARE CONDUCTED BY THE WHOLE HOUSEHOLD.

BIRTH

Because Athenian law decrees that property must be shared equally between all sons, large families are not favoured in Attica. However, infanticide is illegal, and abortion may only be practised with the permission of the father. An unwanted child may be exposed at birth, and such children are often rescued, although only to be raised as slaves.

Infant mortality is high, so the parents wait one week to perform the *amphidromia*, the ceremony to cleanse the house and mother of blood pollution. The father then carries the baby around the hearth. If you are invited to the celebration banquet ten days after the birth, you will be expected to bring a gift.

MARRIAGE

After infancy, girls and boys are raised separately, with the girls secluded in the gynaikeion. Hence, there is little chance for the sexes to mix and for relationships to develop of their own accord.

A marriage is arranged between the fathers, without the presence or consent of their children, and the couple is betrothed as soon as the fathers agree terms. A boy marries after he has finished his ephebia between the ages of 20 and 30, and a girl at 14 or 15. The most popular

The bride and groom often meet for the first time on their wedding day.

GRAVE MARKERS

Athenians mark their graves with stone funerary monuments. In ancient times, these were sphinxes and kouroi, but recently elaborate carved statues and reliefs of the deceased have become popular. The main cemeteries of Athens are to be found in the Outer Kerameikos district.

time of year for weddings is the month of Gamelion, when Father Zeus married Mother Hera.

On the eve of the wedding, the bride and groom each take a ritual bath. Both houses are decorated with olive and laurel boughs. On the afternoon of the wedding, the groom goes to the bride's house accompanied by his family and friends. The wedding banquet is usually the first time the bride and groom meet, and afterwards they will ride to the groom's home in an open carriage, accompanied by the guests singing, dancing and playing music. They are showered with nuts and figs as they cross the hearth. They go straight to the bridal chamber, and their friends stand guard outside, making noise and singing to ward off evil.

OLD AGE AND DEATH

Like all Greeks, the Athenians respect and honour their elders, and a son is expected to give his parents a proper funeral.

When a family member dies, he or she is taken from the city before sunrise to the family grave in one of the cemeteries outside the city walls. The mourners wear black or grey, and carry white *leukythoi* (vessels for libations of oil and wine).

The body is either buried or cremated, and the remains are placed under a grave marker. A funerary feast is held after the burial. Because death is held to pollute all who come into contact with it, mourners must be ritually cleansed before they can return to normal life.

CLOTHING AND DRESS

UNLIKE THE BARBARIANS OF EGYPT, THE LEVANT AND PERSIA, THE GREEKS ARE NOT OSTENTATIOUS IN THEIR DRESS. MEN AND WOMEN WEAR PLAIN WOOLLEN GARMENTS, AND, UNLESS VERY WEALTHY, FEW ACCESSORIES AND JEWELLERY. ALTHOUGH WOMEN ARE EXPECTED TO BE MODESTLY DRESSED AT ALL TIMES, AND ARE USUALLY COVERED FROM HEAD TO TOE WHEN IN PUBLIC, YOUNG MEN, ESPECIALLY THOSE CONSIDERED TO BE PARTICULARLY ATTRACTIVE AND ATHLETIC, SEEK EVERY OPPORTUNITY TO SHOW OFF THEIR PHYSICAL FORM.

Although Athenians spend lavishly on glorifying their gods, ostentatious display in the form either of interior decoration or their own personal adornment is discouraged.

Attic garments are made of homespun cloth – wool for the winter and linen for the summer – that is dyed in bright colours or bleached white, and cut or sewn into a few simple shapes at home by the women of the house. While modesty is expected of women at all times, men often disport themselves in just a *himation* (cloak), and even go nude at the gymnasium and during dance and athletics contests.

CLOTHING

The principle garment for men in Greece is the *chiton*, a sleeveless tunic that reaches the knee or calf, and is belted with a *zone* or a broader leather belt called a *zoster*. The chiton can be worn with the *chlamys*, an oblong of dyed material worn as a short cape, or the larger himation. A plain himation of coarse wool is called a *trebon*.

Slaves, labourers and soldiers wear the *exomis*, a tunic that leaves one shoulder uncovered. At night

Attic clothing is simple and functional.

*Athenian men and women
style their hair carefully.*

WHAT TO EXPECT

HAIRSTYLES

Both Attic men and women are careful to clean, style and perfume their hair. Hair curling is popular, as are perfumed lotions and waxes.

Women wear their hair long, in braids, ponytails or piled up on top of the head. It is kept in place by intricate ribbon or metal headbands.

Men wear their hair long or short, and older men have a full beard, the symbol of adulthood. Serving soldiers, however, are expected to be clean-shaven.

a belt. When out of the house, women are expected to veil themselves modestly with their himation. When travelling, they carry a *skiadion*, or parasol. Wealthy men and women wear gold and silver jewellery, including hairpins, earrings, necklaces, rings and brooches, and carry fans.

FOOTWEAR

Indoors most go unshod, but outdoors those who can afford to wear sandals or high lace-up boots known as *embas*. Women wear brightly dyed shoes and sandals, and sometimes increase their height by inserting a layer of cork or leather inside the shoe. Slaves, labourers and members of the poorer classes go about barefoot.

the men remove their belts and sleep in their tunics.

Greek travellers will tuck their chiton into their belt, leaving their legs unencumbered for walking. In winter, they wrap themselves in their himatia, which are also used in lieu of bedclothes at inns.

Women's clothing is not very different from men's, though it is generally more colourful. Women also wear the chiton or, in colder weather, the floor-length peplos, both gathered at the waist with

HEADGEAR

In town men do not usually wear hats, and women cover their heads with their himation; but when travelling, men wear the broad-brimmed *petasos* and women, the *tholia*, to ward off the sun or rain.

FOOD AND DRINK

 THE TRADITIONAL ATTIC DIET IS PROBABLY ONE OF THE POOREST IN MAINLAND GREECE. IT CONSISTS MAINLY OF BREAD, EATEN WITH OLIVES, ONIONS, LENTILS AND LEEKS, WITH SOME CHEESE OR FISH, AND MEAT ONLY ON FEAST DAYS. BUT OF LATE, THE EXPANSION OF TRADE HAS IMPROVED THE VARIETY OF FOOD AVAILABLE. THE MARKETS OF ATHENS AND PIRAEUS NOW STOCK COMESTIBLES FROM THE FOUR CORNERS OF THE KNOWN WORLD, WHICH, THOUGH EXPENSIVE, ARE AVAILABLE IN INNS AND TAVERNS.

GRAIN-EATERS

Even in blind Homer's day, the Greeks were known as 'grain-eaters', and among the modern Greeks, the name particularly suits the Athenians. The staple of the Attic diet is still grain: for the poor, barley, made into flat cakes on the griddle, known as *maza*; and for the well-to-do, oven-baked loaves

---

WHAT TO EXPECT

BEVERAGES

The common beverage served with meals is good fresh spring water, sometimes mixed with honey, when it is known as *hydromel*. The milk of goats and sheep is available in the country, but it is wine, 'the gift of Dionysos', that is the most popular drink by far.

Wine is produced all over Attica, but especially in the Mesogeia; however, it is also imported in large earthenware amphorae from other Greek cities, the Aegean islands, Ionian Asia, and even from Magna Graecia. Attic wine is preserved by the addition of salt water, and is flavoured with herbs and spices, especially thyme, pennyroyal and cinnamon.

made of wheaten flour, known as *artos*. In the countryside, *kykeon*, porridge made of barley meal and flavoured with herbs, in particular thyme, is a popular alternative to maza. Doctors are apt to prescribe this dish for the sick and elderly.

Although in olden days each family made its own bread, loaves can now be purchased from bakeries in the main demes. All solid food served as an accompaniment to bread is known as *opson*. This includes olives, onions, leeks, garlic, beans and lentils, which are plentiful and cheap, and imported green vegetables, which are scarce and dear. Beans and lentils are also eaten mashed into a thick soup called *etnos*, of which, it is said, the mighty Herakles was fond.

EATING MEAT

Meat is a luxury in Attica, especially beef, as cattle are rare here. The most affordable meat is pork, and a suckling pig can be had for two drachmas, which is still dear at a day's wages for a skilled workman.

However, those taking part in a religious festival are entitled to a cut of meat from the sacrifice offered to the god. During the Greater Panathenaic hekatombion (see p. 103), a hundred oxen are sacrificed to Athena, and much of the meat is distributed among those present.

When travelling through the countryside, your diet will be more varied, as mutton, goat, fowl and wild game are also available.

With meat in short supply, Athenians often have fish as their main opson. Anchovies and sardines – plentiful in local waters – are particular favourites, but you will also find sea eels, shellfish, octopus and squid.

In Athens, the fish market is one of the most colourful and crowded in the Agora. If you are in one of the coastal demes, make your way to the harbour early in the morning to buy the pick of the day's catch straight off the boat. Freshwater fish is also relished, in particular freshwater eels.

WEIGHTS, MEASURES AND MONEY

ATHENS PLAYS SUCH AN IMPORTANT ROLE IN THE WORLD TRADING SYSTEM THAT ITS CURRENCY, THE SILVER DRACHMA, AND THE TRADITIONAL ATTIC WEIGHTS AND MEASURES HAVE BECOME STANDARDS ACROSS THE MIDDLE SEA AND BEYOND. ARRIVING IN ATHENS, IF YOU ARE NOT CARRYING ATHENIAN 'OWLS', YOU WILL HAVE TO CONVERT YOUR OWN CURRENCY INTO THE LOCAL OBOL AND DRACHMA. AS FOR MOST THINGS IN ATHENS, YOUR FIRST STOP IS THE AGORA.

MONEY MATTERS

One of the major headaches of travel is the ever-present danger of being robbed. However, the traveller must carry a well-filled purse to cover expenses for the entire trip. For security, you would be well advised to travel in a group, or take along several trusted slaves as bodyguards.

In addition to the Attic drachma, there are two currencies that are widely traded in Greece: the Persian gold daric and the electrum stater from Cyzicus in Asian Ionia. In Athens, however, you will be expected to pay for lodgings and purchases in the local currency.

Drachma coins carry an image of Athena on the face and that of an owl on the obverse.

If you do not already have *glaukai*, or 'owls' – the nickname given to Attic coins because of the owl they bear – when you arrive in Piraeus or Athens, you should make your way to the *trapezites* ('table men' or moneychangers), who will weigh and assay your coins and exchange them for the equivalent value in Attic coin. In Athens, you will find the trapezites in the South Stoa, and in Piraeus, in the Emporion.

The drachma is a silver currency, and the ores for its minting come from Laureion. The denominations of the drachma are two, four, six, eight and ten, though the most common is the *tetradrachmon* (four-drachma) coin. There are six obols to the drachma, and the obol is further divided into the hemiobol, or half obol. To give you an idea of the purchasing power of the drachma, the average daily wage is between one and two drachmas, and a juror is paid half a drachma for his day's service. The divisions of currency are quite simple: 6 obols = 1 drachma; 100 drachmas = 1 mina; 600 minai = 1 talent.

Athenians carry their money in a purse, in the folds of their clothing, or often, under their tongue, where it is difficult for a pickpocket to reach!

Bronze coins have recently been introduced to Attica, as subdivisions of the obol, but are rare, and as of the time of writing no official conversion rate has been fixed with the drachma. You are best advised to stick to silver or gold for your transactions.

Weights and Measures

The commercial weights of Athens are closely related to currency, as both represent the weight of a commodity. In the case of currency, this is bronze, silver, electrum or gold, but similar terms of obols, drachmas, minai and talents are also applied to weights of other goods. The basic unit of dry volume is the choenix, or a day's corn ration for a man: 4 cotylai = 1 choenix; 8 choeniches = 1 hecteus; 6 hecteis = 1 medimnos.

As with dry volumes, there is a basic unit to measure liquid commodities, the metretes, which is equivalent to one wine amphora. 6 cotylai = 1 hemichous; 12 cotylai = 1 chous; 12 choes = 1 metretes.

The measurements of length are based on various parts of the human body, the finger, hand, arm and foot: 1 dactylos = 1 fingerwidth; 16 dactyloi = 1 pode (foot); 600 pedes = 1 stadion.

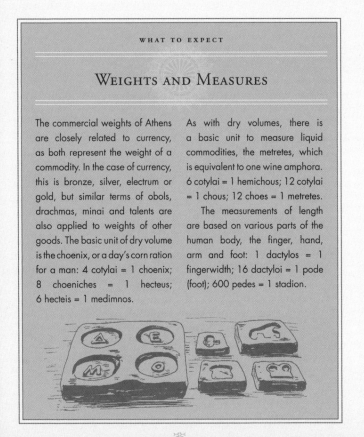

SHOPPING

ATHENS AND PIRAEUS ARE TRULY THE MARKETPLACES OF GREECE, WITH PRODUCE FLOWING IN FROM MAGNA GRAECIA, EGYPT, THE LEVANT AND THE BLACK SEA, MUCH OF IT FOR RESALE TO OTHER GREEK STATES. IN ADDITION TO FOREIGN GOODS, YOU WILL FIND HERE THE WORLD'S FINEST CERAMICS — BOTH FUNCTIONAL AND DECORATIVE — LEATHERWARES, AND PARTICULARLY FINE BRONZE- AND METALWORK. FOR ALL THINGS FOREIGN, GO TO PIRAEUS, BUT FOR ATHENIAN PURCHASES, HEAD TO THE AGORA AND ITS SURROUNDING WORKSHOPS.

WHERE TO GO

The markets in Athens and Piraeus are the largest and most cosmopolitan in Greece, eclipsing their former commercial rivals Aegina and Corinth.

Imported goods arrive at the Emporion (see p. 81) in Piraeus, where they are sold on to Greek merchants for re-export, or to local merchants who will take them to Athens and other Attic demes.

Manufactures and produce from nearby, however, are sold in the Hippodemeia, the agora of Piraeus. No such distinction exists in Athens, and all goods, from agricultural produce to the finest works of tekne, are for sale in the Agora. The Agora is subdivided

---

WHAT TO EXPECT

COMMISSIONING A VOTIVE OFFERING

Since the Periklean building programme began, Athens has become home to Greece's best stone workers and sculptors. The temples contain the works of the masters; but there are also more modest workshops, from which you can commission a votive offering in bronze or marble to dedicate to your favourite deity.

CERAMIC SOUVENIRS

Attica has plentiful supplies of fine potter's clay that fires to a rich red-orange colour. The Athenians learned the black-figure decorative technique from Corinth in the Archaic period. Around a century ago, Athenian potters reversed colours of the ground and figures to produce the first red-figure wares. Pieces are painted with scenes of daily life, battle and athletic contests, as well as religious and historical subjects.

Typical shapes for decorative wares include the two-handled amphora, the *hydria* (water jar), the *krater*, for mixing wine and water, the *kylix* (shallow cup), the *rhyton*, a horn-shaped drinking vessel, as well as ewers, and also *leukythoi* (funerary wares).

Large red-figure amphorae are often given as wedding presents, and they are also awarded as prizes during the Panathenaic Games.

into several areas: for meat, fish, wine, fruit and vegetables, spices, and for the different manufactured goods and imported luxuries. A slave market is held here monthly on the day of the new moon.

In addition to temporary market stalls, craftsmen have their shops and workshops in the immediate vicinity of the Agora: metalworkers around the temple of Hephaistos, potters in the Kerameikos, and leatherworkers, basket makers and furniture makers on the north and east sides.

WHAT TO BUY

Athens is known for the quality of her olive oil, though this is scarcer since the outbreak of the war with Sparta, and the yearly attacks of the enemy who destroy the olive groves in a vain attempt to cripple the Athenian economy. Wine is also produced in the Mesogeia (see pp. 96–7), but again production has been hindered by the war.

The two manufactures for which Athens is best known are her metalwork, in particular bronze, and her ceramic wares.

BATHS AND BATHING

THE ATTIC GREEKS ARE CLEAN ABOUT THEIR PERSON AND USUALLY WELL GROOMED. AS ONLY THE LARGER HOUSES HAVE BATHROOMS — USUALLY A SUBDIVISION OF THE KITCHEN — MOST ATHENIANS GO TO THE PUBLIC BATHS, WHICH ARE COMMON IN THE URBAN DEMES. IN THE RURAL AND COASTAL DEMES, YOU MAY HAVE TO MAKE DO WITH THE LOCAL RIVER, LAKE OR SEA, BUT IN THE WARM ATTIC CLIMATE THIS IS NO REAL HARDSHIP. WHERE THE ATHENIANS DO FALL SHORT, AS FAR AS THE TRAVELLER IS CONCERNED, IS IN THE COMPLETE ABSENCE OF PUBLIC LAVATORIES.

Public baths can be found in all major Attic towns.

IN THE PRIVATE HOUSE

If you are a guest in a well-to-do home you will find the bathroom next to the kitchen. The nearness of the stove makes it easy to carry hot water to the bathroom, which is equipped with a terracotta hipbath in which you sit, or a stone or terracotta basin on a pedestal. The great physician Hippocrates (see p. 139) recommends sitting rather than reclining in the bath, and, like the hardy Spartans, he is also very enthusiastic about the health-giving properties of cold baths.

It is customary for a host to offer his guest a bath as soon as he or she arrives. As a rule, Athenians bathe before sitting down to their evening meal.

AT THE GYM

Public bathing facilities are also available at public gymnasia (for Athens, see pp. 76–7). At the better-appointed gyms, baths can be sizeable, with excellent facilities. A new device recently introduced to the gymnasium baths is the 'shower'. A refreshing stream of water is released by a slave from a tank above the bather through an opening made in the shape of an animal head.

PUBLIC BATHS

If you are staying in a house without a bathroom or at an inn, you will have to use one of the many public baths found in all the urban demes of Attica.

Arriving at the baths, undress in the dressing room. Make sure that you bring a slave with you, or that you can keep an eye on your belongings at all times, because theft from public baths is endemic, and the management declines any responsibility for stolen property.

In the bath proper, you may have an individual tub or the attendant may slosh water over you from a communal basin. Bathhouses provide *rhymma* (cleanser), which can be lye, grease mixed with wood ash, or fuller's earth, but they do not provide a *stlengis* (scraper), towel or oil, which you will need to bring yourself. In some of the larger establishments you will also find a steam bath as well as a cold plunge pool.

Once you have washed with the rhymma, you or your slave will scrape it off with the stlengis. Once you have rinsed again or gone for a steam bath and cold plunge, you should towel yourself dry, and anoint yourself with aromatic oil.

LAVATORIES

There are no public lavatories in Athens or in the major urban demes, which means that, if you are out for the day, you'll have to relieve yourself as best you can. Indoors – even in the grander houses – you will only find terracotta chamber pots or buckets that are emptied at regular intervals by the house slaves. The sudden emptying of chamber pots is a hazard of walking the narrow streets of Athens.

CRIME AND THE LAW

THE LAWS OF ATTICA ARE HARSH FOR THOSE FOUND GUILTY OF CRIMES AGAINST THE PERSON AND THE STATE. THE MILDEST CRIMES CARRY FINANCIAL PUNISHMENTS, BUT THE MOST SERIOUS ARE PUNISHABLE BY DEATH. IN ADDITION TO THE CORPS OF SCYTHIAN SLAVE ARCHERS EMPLOYED TO MAINTAIN PUBLIC ORDER, THE CITY HAS ELEVEN CRIMINAL COMMISSIONERS WHO OVERSEE THE ARREST, IMPRISONMENT AND PUNISHMENT OF CRIMINALS.

A criminal who is caught in the act of robbing, assaulting, murdering or raping can expect to receive summary justice from any apprehending citizen. The criminal will be executed on the spot: clubbed to death, stoned or cast from the heights of the Acropolis.

Otherwise he will be handed over to the Criminal Commissioners, who take him to the state prison near the Agora, and arraign him for trial.

The offence decides the court a malefactor will be taken to. It is the King Archon who tries

---

WHAT TO EXPECT

KNOW YOUR PROXENOS

If you are staying in Athens for any length of time, it would be wise to inquire as to the identity and whereabouts of your home state's *proxenos*.

The proxenos is an Athenian or metic charged with looking after the interests of another Greek city-state. The post is unpaid and is therefore held by wealthy men

of influence. The noble Alkibiades, for example, soon to depart for the expedition to Sicily, is the proxenos of Sparta.

Your proxenos can help you with a loan if you are short of money, with legal aid if you become embroiled in a lawsuit, or even, more straightforwardly, with tickets for seats at the theatre.

The juice of the hemlock plant is used as a means of execution.

murderers and blasphemers; the Eponymous Archon oversees civil suits brought by citizens; and the Archon Polemarch, cases involving metics and foreigners. Other courts include the Delphinion (see p. 61) for cases of homicide that are claimed to be justified, and the Phreatto (see p. 81) for manslaughter and homicide cases concerning citizens who have been banished and, of course, many cases are heard by the jury courts of the Heliaia (see p. 67), where the plaintiff and accused each plead their own causes, and the jury decides first the verdict then the sentence.

PUNISHMENT

Once convicted, the criminal is handed back to the Criminal Commissioners, who will enforce the sentence of the court. The mildest penalties are financial – fines, damages and confiscation of property. Next in severity are temporary banishment from the city, loss of civic rights (that is, the right to vote in the Ekklesia, hold office, and be eligible for jury service) and permanent exile. The physical punishments – whipping, branding and the *xyla*, or pillory, are reserved for slaves.

Those convicted of murder, treason and piracy are subject to the death penalty. For the most fortunate, a brew of deadly hemlock is administered in prison. Death is painful but quick and private. Other offenders are taken to the place of execution along the Northern Long Wall, where they are pegged out on wooden boards with five iron clamps around their wrists, ankles and neck, and left there to die slowly and painfully of thirst – a punishment that is meted out to traitors, rebels and pirates. When the island of Samos rebelled against Athenian rule, Perikles had Samians pegged out in the agora of Samos and left them there to die as an example to the others.

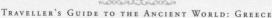
IF YOU ARE ILL

ILL HEALTH IS ONE OF THE PERILS OF TRAVEL. WHILE MANY STILL BELIEVE THAT SICKNESS IS A CURSE SENT BY THE GODS TO PUNISH MORTALS, AND WILL SEEK CURES BY MAKING SACRIFICES AT THEIR ALTARS, THERE IS A NEW SCHOOL OF MEDICINE IN GREECE — THE HIPPOCRATIC SCHOOL — THAT REJECTS SUCH EXPLANATION AND SEEKS NATURAL CAUSES FOR DISEASE. WHICHEVER YOU HOLD TO BE TRUE, YOU WILL BE WELL CARED FOR IN ATHENS, WHICH HAS NO SHORTAGE OF DOCTORS, AS WELL AS AN IMPORTANT SHRINE TO ASKLEPIOS AND HYGIEIA.

While it is never good to succumb to illness, at least the traveller to Athens is fortunate that the city has many healers, magical practitioners and doctors, as well as a sanctuary of Asklepios and Hygieia. In addition to her private and state doctors, Athens has a number of specialists in dentistry and ocular medicine, and skilled surgeons.

THE GOD OF DREAMS

Although Asklepios' main temple is in the city of Epidauros in the Pelopponnese, some five years ago a private citizen of Athens by the name of Telemakhos 'brought the god back' with him to the city, and built the Asklepeion (see p. 58) on the south slope of the Acropolis next to the theatre of Dionysos.

Like all of the god's shrines, the site is associated with a sacred spring that flows from the living rock, and it also has a *bothros*, or canopied pit, in which the sacred snakes are kept.

The sanctuary is not large, having only a small naos and a stoa with no more than three rooms.

CONSULTING THE GOD

If you wish to consult the god about an illness, you must present yourself at the temple and make an offering to him and his daughter Hygieia.

The priest will lead you to the sacred spring to drink the waters and bathe. He will then take you to the bothros to meet the god in his animal form. Then you will be taken to the neighbouring stoa to

The Hippocratic School

Hippokrates of Kos teaches a revolutionary doctrine about the causes of disease and their cure. He rejects the idea that it is the gods who send plagues to punish men for their sins, and instead looks to natural phenomena, such as the environment or poor diet and lifestyle as the causes for imbalances in the four 'humours': blood, black bile, yellow bile and phlegm. If the humours are in a state of *dyskrasia*, or 'bad mixture', a person will fall ill and can only be restored to health with proper care that restores the humours to their rightful balance.

The therapeutic approach of the school is gentle, however, as it teaches that in most cases the body will heal itself, as long as the patient is kept clean, immobile and quiet. Hippokrates does not give strong drugs or treatments lightly because of the danger of misdiagnosis, preferring instead to prescribe changes in diet, baths and exercise. This approach suits some ailments well – broken bones, for example, benefit from immobility, and Hippokrates has devised a bench that holds the bones in place as they heal.

Hippokrates and his followers are excellent diagnosticians, and can even tell some patient's illnesses from examining their hands.

sleep to await the visitation of the god in your dreams, so that he can prescribe a cure.

While the visitor is sleeping the god may appear to them in order to ask his supplicant to fast, bathe or perhaps to make further offerings on his altar. Visitors should note that it is said to be especially propitious if he visits your dreams in the form of a serpent.

HYGIEIA

It is also worth noting that Asklepios' daughter, the goddess of health and cleanliness, Hygieia is also worshipped in the shrine.

Her statue is to be found in the small temple that is situated next to that of her divine father.

STUDYING IN ATHENS

ATHENS IS KNOWN THROUGHOUT THE WORLD AS THE CITY OF THE ARTS AND CULTURE, SO IT IS PERHAPS STRANGE THAT THERE ARE FEW SCHOOLS HERE, AND THAT THE ATHENIAN FATHER IS FREE TO EDUCATE HIS CHILDREN IN WHATEVER WAY BEST PLEASES HIM. THE CITY, HOWEVER, IS A MAGNET FOR MANY GREAT THINKERS AND TEACHERS WHO YOU CAN LISTEN TO IN THE AGORA AND THE GYMNASIA. YOU MAY EVEN ENGAGE SOME AS PRIVATE TUTORS — ALTHOUGH YOU MAY NEED A DEEP PURSE IF YOU ARE TO EMPLOY SOME OF THE GREATEST MINDS OF ATHENS.

SOPHISTS

The word *sophos* means wisdom, so the term *sophistes* can be applied to artists, especially poets, dramatists and musicians, and also to experts in any craft or occupation. In the field of education, however, it refers to men who travel from city to city and who specialise in teaching the arts of oratory.

In Athens, where so much is decided in the Ekklesia and in the jury courts, a talent with words is highly prized; hence those who claim to be able to teach it are much sought after.

Whether the sophists are truly worth the high fees they charge is a matter open to debate. There are many, such as the disciples of

PROTAGORAS

A native of Abdera in Thrace, Protagoras was the first of the great sophists to come to teach in Athens. He was admired by Sokrates and was a friend and confidant of Perikles, with whom he would converse on matters of law, virtue and government. An agnostic in matters of religion, his most famous saying is, 'Man is the measure of all things: of things which are, that they are, and of things which are not, that they are not.'

SOKRATES

The playwright Aristophanes has portrayed Sokrates in one of his comedies as a sophist, but it is unlikely that he himself would accept the title.

Without doubt the greatest thinker and philosopher of the age, and a man of unparalleled intelligence and erudition, he never asks for fees from his pupils. He cites his own poverty as proof that he is not a sophist. You can see him by day walking barefoot in the Agora, where he will sit in the shade of one of the stoas to lecture and question his students, or taking his ease at one of the city's gymnasia. It is said that the Akademeia (see p. 76) is his favourite.

Questioning is at the very heart of his teaching method, and his questions are so relentless that the student is either struck dumb or forced to develop a sudden insight about the topic under discussion.

In his private life, although a married man with three sons, he is also a great admirer of young athletes, and though short and ugly (a fact he readily accepts), he is always surrounded by the most handsome and the wealthiest of Athens' aristocratic youth, and is a regular guest at their symposia where he pays for his wine with his undoubted wisdom and wit.

The foremost philosopher of the age is the Athenian Sokrates.

Sokrates, who denounce them as money-grubbing men whose honeyed words mask unprincipled souls. However, Sokrates himself has paid homage to Protagoras of Abdera, who was one of the greatest sophists to teach in Athens and who was an associate of Perikles. Sokrates has even been known to send several of his own students to train with a sophist.

Be warned, however, that if the purpose of your visit to Athens is to study and learn with one of the sophists who now live in the city, you must be wealthy in the extreme, and the wine must flow freely at your table. The best place to meet both sophists and philosophers in full flow is at one of the many symposia that are held in the city.

REFERENCES
AND RESOURCES

Although there is much to see and do in Athens,
your visit can only be enhanced by a deeper
understanding of this unique city-state. With this
aim in mind you will find a list of famous Athenians,
some recommended reading, notes on the
Greek alphabet and numbers, and some useful
terms and phrases included to make your stay
all the more enjoyable.

SOME FAMOUS ATHENIANS

AS BEFITS SUCH A FAMOUS CITY, ATHENS HAS BORNE MANY FAMOUS SONS. AND NOT ONLY IS THE CITY FAMED FOR ITS MONUMENTS, CUSTOMS AND ACHIEVEMENTS, BUT ALSO FOR THOSE WHO FIRST INSTITUTED THEM. OF THE MANY ILLUSTRIOUS ATHENIANS WHOSE NAMES ARE CERTAIN TO ECHO THROUGHOUT THE AGES, THERE IS SPACE TO DETAIL ONLY A FEW BELOW.

DRAKO

The great lawgiver, who lived two centuries ago, was the first to codify the laws of Attica and make them known to all citizens. This code of laws, however, was extremely harsh, and even minor offences were punishable by the death penalty.

SOLON

The second of Attica's great lawgivers was Solon, who served as Eponymous Archon a little under 200 years ago. During his term of office he tried to reconcile the warring factions that were threatening to destroy the state. He is remembered as the 'father of democracy' because he increased the participation in the Ekklesia and created the court of the Heliaia and the first Boule.

PEISISTRATOS

On three occasions in the previous century, Peisistratos was *tyrannos* (tyrant) of Athens. Appointed under

Solon: the 'father of democracy', and creator of the court of the Heliaia and the first Boule.

martial law, he represented the party of the rural poor, with whose backing he seized and maintained power. He favoured the common people over the aristocracy and kept Solon's democratic reforms. He embellished the city with temples and civic buildings, improved the city's water supply and laid out the Lykeion.

KLEISTHENES

Although he was of noble birth, Kleisthenes was one of the greatest stalwarts of Athenian democracy.

He overthrew the tyranny of Hippias, son and successor of Peisistratos, and reformed the Athenian constitution. He called his reforms *isonomia* (equality of political rights) rather than *demokratia*. He replaced the four traditional phyllai with ten new tribes, created the 139 demes, increased the Boule to 500 and reformed the jury system.

MILTIADES

A former vassal of Darios I of Persia, Miltiades joined the Ionian revolt against Persia a little under a century ago. He fled to Athens when the revolt was crushed, and was subsequently elected strategos. He is most famous for devising the tactics that won the Greeks victory against the odds at the battle of Marathon.

KIMON

The leader of the aristocratic party, Kimon was a distinguished soldier, holding the posts of strategos and of fleet admiral.

Ostracised (see p. 19) a little under 50 years ago on suspicion of having treasonable dealings with Sparta, he was recalled before the end of his exile to mediate the five-year truce with the Spartans some ten years later.

EPHIALTES

The leader of the democratic faction and the patron of Perikles, Ephialtes reformed the Council of the Aeropagos (see p. 20), transferring many of its powers to the Boule, Ekklesia and the jury courts. These reforms were the foundations for the later democratic constitution.

PERIKLES

The leader of the democratic party, Perikles was Attica's leading citizen from the murder of Ephialtes to the time of his own death from the plague just 14 years before the time of writing. Although of aristocratic stock, he was a champion of democracy. He commissioned the rebuilding of the temples of the Acropolis and many other buildings in Attica.

THEMISTOKLES

He famously persuaded the Ekklesia to spend the silver discovered at Laureion (see p. 88) on expanding the Athenian fleet from 70 to 200 triremes, an act that saved Athens and all Greece.

After the destruction of Athens in the first Persian invasion, he supervised the building of the city walls and fortified the port of Piraeus. He died in exile, but his remains were brought back to Attica and buried at the entrance to Kantharos harbour in Piraeus.

RECOMMENDED READING

THE TRAVELLER TO GREECE AND ATHENS IN
PARTICULAR WOULD BE WISE TO VERSE THEMSELVES
IN THE EPICS OF THE ILIAD AND THE ODYSSEY;
THESE ARE THE BEDROCK OF GREEK LITERATURE,
AND INFORM THE GREEK MINDSET.

Greek literature is founded upon the epic, the greatest examples of which are the *Iliad* and the *Odyssey*. The central themes of the *Iliad* are tragic and heroic, and describe the actions of the Greeks and Trojans during the Trojan War; of course, the involvement of the immortal gods is central. The *Odyssey* is the somewhat lighter, albeit still epic tale of Odysseus' homeward voyage.

On a more prosaic note the works of Herodotos (Herodotus) provide great insight into day-to-day life.

* The modern reader should note that a full picture of ancient Greek literature can only be understood with reference to later writers; for example, the thoughts of Sokrates are unveiled by his students Plato and Xenophon in their later work, *The Sokratic Dialogues*.

HERODOTOS

A native of Halicarnassus in Asian Ionia, Herodotos is regarded as the first true Western historian. He wrote his *Histories* between ten years and 15 years ago. The greater part of the book deals with the origins of the war between the Greeks and Persians.

He himself was a great traveller, visiting most of the Oikoumene, or the known world of his day. His writings are full of digressions and

anecdotes that enliven what would otherwise be a dry political and military account. The first sections of the *Histories* deal with the rise of the Persian Empire under Cyrus the Great. He then moves on to the conquest of Egypt before turning his attention to the revolt of the Asian Ionians, which triggered the war between Persia and Greece. The book closes with the Persian defeats at Salamis and Plataia.

GREEK LETTERS AND NUMBERS

In the most ancient times, the Greeks of Mycenae used the script of Minoan Crete, and these letters, whose meaning is now lost, can still be seen on the buildings, tombs and artefacts of the period. The alphabet in common use in Greece today is based on the Phoenician writing system. The Greeks have 24 letters in their alphabet, and they use another three obsolete letters as part of their number system.

Ancient Greek has seven vowels: A (alpha) is pronounced 'o' as in 'not'; E (epsilon) as the 'ay' in 'bay'; H (eta) as the 'e' in 'bet'; I (iota) as the 'ee' in 'see'; O (omicron) as 'o' in 'no'; Y (upsilon) as 'oo' in 'too'; and finally W (omega) is pronounced like the 'aw' in 'awe'.

Most of its 17 consonants will be familiar to the reader apart from Q (theta), pronounced 'th'; C (xi), pronounced 'x' as in 'box'; X (chi), a hard 'kh' sound; and Y (psi), pronounced 'ps' as 'lapse'.

Greek characters also have a second use, as, apart from a single upward stroke for the number one, the Greeks do not have separate characters or ciphers to represent their numerals. Instead they use the letters of the alphabet. Each is assigned a numerical value, so that, for example, the letter alpha also stands for the number one, beta for two, gamma for three, and so on. Three obsolete letters (not shown) are used for the numbers 6, 90 and 900.

Greek letters are based on the Phoenician alphabet used in the Levant.

A	α	*alpha*
B	β	*beta*
Γ	γ	*gamma*
Δ	δ	*delta*
E	ε	*epsilon*
Z	ζ	*zeta*
H	η	*eta*
Θ	θ	*theta*
I	ι	*iota*
K	κ	*kappa*
Λ	λ	*lambda*
M	μ	*mu*
N	ν	*nu*
Ξ	ξ	*xi*
O	o	*omicron*
Π	π	*pi*
P	ρ	*rho*
Σ	σ ς	*sigma*
T	τ	*tau*
Y	υ	*upsilon*
Φ	φ	*phi*
X	χ	*chi*
Ψ	ψ	*psi*
Ω	ω	*omega*

RECOMMENDED VIEWING

ONE OF THE BEST WAYS TO UNDERSTAND LIFE IN ATHENS IS TO TAKE IN ONE OF THE TRAGIC OR COMIC DRAMAS PERFORMED AT THE DIONYSIA AND LENAIA (SEE PP. 106–9), NOT LEAST THE TRAGEDIES PENNED BY AESKHYLOS, SOPHOKLES AND EURIPIDES, AND THE COMEDIES BY ARISTOPHANES. THE TRAGEDIES, WHICH DEAL WITH LOFTY POLITICAL AND PHILOSOPHICAL THEMES, ARE INFORMATIVE ON THE SUBJECT OF THE IDEALS AND BELIEFS OF THE ATHENIANS, WHILE THE COMEDIES, WITH THEIR BAWDY HUMOUR AND TOPICAL THEMES, ARE MUCH MORE REVEALING ABOUT THE LIVES OF THE COMMON PEOPLE.

TRAGEDY AND COMEDY

The tragedies on show in Athens often revolve around well-known stories. These provide a useful insight into the complex system of values and beliefs held by the Athenian people.

Aeskhylos, a veteran of the battle of Marathon, whose plays include *The Persians*, and also the tragic trilogy *The Oresteia* (see box); Sophokles, whose plays include *Oedipus the King*; and Euripides, whose plays include *The Bacchae*, are the most notable of the tragic playwrights.

Although on a much lighter note, comedies can also provide useful insights into life in Athens. For example, *The Acharnians*, Aristophanes' first play, with which he won first prize in the comedic competition of the Lenaia at the age of 20. In his subsequent long

A scene from The Oresteia *by Aeskhylos,*
the greatest tragic trilogy ever written.

TRAGEDIES OF BLOOD

Acknowledged by many to be the greatest tragic trilogy ever written for the Greek stage, *The Oresteia* by Aeskhylos won first prize at the City Dionysia when it was first performed. The three plays deal with the curse on the House of Atreus, the ruling family of the city of Argos.

In the first play, *Agamemnon*, the returning conqueror of Troy is murdered by his wife, Clytemnestra, in revenge for the sacrifice of their daughter, Iphigeneia, which the gods had demanded in order to allow the Greek fleet to sail to Asia. Adding insult to injury, Clytemnestra and her lover Aegisthus usurp the throne, exiling Agamemnon's son Orestes. In the second play, *The Libation Bearers*, Agamemnon's and Clytemnestra's disinherited children, Orestes and Elektra, are reunited and avenge their father's murder by killing their mother and her lover. Orestes is pursued by the avenging Furies to Athens, where in the third play, *The Eumenides*, he faces trial by jury for his crime. The jury of twelve Athenians presided over by Athena returns a hung verdict, and it is up to the goddess to persuade the Furies to acquit the murderer. After she succeeds, the avenging Furies are renamed the *Eumenides*, or 'the Kindly Ones', and a shrine is built for their veneration in Athens on the rock of the Areopagos.

---

career, he has remained one of the most popular playwrights in Athens and a trenchant critic of the Spartan war and the abuses of Athens' political leaders.

In *The Acharnians* Dikaepolis speaks up in the Ekklesia against the Spartan war but is ignored. Undeterred, he decides to sign a private peace with the enemy, for which he is condemned by the warlike Acharnians. With the playwright Euripides' help, he manages to sway the Acharnians to his side and begins to trade with the enemy. The play ends in a set-piece farce with Dikaepolis enriched and his enemies humbled.

The Knights, which is another comedy by Aristophanes, delivers a savage attack on Kleon, Perikles' successor as head of the democratic party. Lampooned as the steward for the not very bright Demos (a personification of the people of Athens), Kleon is challenged for power by a lowly sausage-seller, who promises Demos that he can be more tyrannical and unjust. But as soon as he obtains the job, the sausage-seller negotiates peace with Sparta instead.

USEFUL TERMS AND PHRASES

GETTING A GRIP ON THE LOCAL LANGUAGE IS KEY TO YOUR ENJOYMENT OF YOUR STAY. WHETHER HAGGLING IN AN AGORA OR MAKING YOUR POINT AT A SYMPOSION, A LITTLE GREEK WILL GO A LONG WAY.

USEFUL WORDS

Amphora *A ceramic wine jar*

Andron *Men's quarters*

Apobates *A chariot race held during the Greater Panathenaia on the Agora*

Archon *Magistrate of Athens*

Arkteia *'Playing the bear', rite performed at the shrine of Artemis Brauronia*

Arrhephoroi *The child priestesses of Athena Polias*

Artos *Wheat bread*

Aulos *A wind instrument*

Basileos *'King', title of one of the three archons of Athens*

Boule *The executive committee of the Ekklesia*

Chiton *A tunic*

Chlamys *An oblong of material worn by men over the chiton*

Choregoi *'Choir-masters', theatrical producers who pay for the staging of the plays*

Deme *One of 139 rural, coastal or urban districts into which Attica is divided*

Drachma *Basic unit of Athenian currency*

Dromos *Racetrack*

Ekklesia *Ruling assembly of the people of Athens*

Ephebia *Two-year military service that Athenian men complete between 18 and 20*

Etnos *Bean or lentil soup*

Glaukai *'Owls' – nickname of the drachma coins that bear the owl, symbol of Athena*

Gynaikeion *Women's quarters*

Hekatombion *Offering of 100 sacrificial victims*

Hekatompedon *'Hundred-footer' – name given to the main cella of the Parthenon, which is 100 pedes long, and holds the image of the goddess*

Herma *Rectangular stone block on which are carved a set of male genitalia and the head of the god Hermes.*

Herms *Markers at entrances and crossroads to bring good luck – 'the Herms' is the northwest corner of the Agora in Athens where many hermai are erected*

Himation *An oblong piece of material worn as a cloak*

Horos *A boundary stone*

Hydria *A water jar*

Karyatid *A statue in the shape of a woman used instead of a columnar support*

Kithara *An instrument resembling a lyre*

Kore *An archaic statue of an idealised woman standing, facing forwards, fully clothed*

Kouros *An archaic statue of an idealised man or youth standing, facing forwards, and naked*

Kykeon *Barley porridge flavoured with herbs*

Maza *Barley cakes*

Metic *A foreign resident*

Metronomos *An inspector of weights and measures*

Mystai *The initiates of the Greater Mysteries of Eleusis*

Naos *The cella or main cult room of a temple*

Nike *A winged victory*

Obol *One sixth of a drachma*

Opisthodomos *The rear porch of a temple*

Opson *Solid food served with bread, including meat, fish and vegetables*

Orchestra *The performance area of a theatre*

Ostracism *The exile of a citizen for ten years*

Ostrakon *A piece of broken pottery on which the names of those to be ostracised are written*

Palaestra *A wrestling ground*

Peplos *A full-length gown worn by Athenian women*

Petasos *A wide-brimmed hat worn by travellers*

Phyllai *The ten tribes of Attica*

Polis *The city-state – both the city itself and the citizens that compose it*

Porneion *A brothel*

Pronaos *A temple's front porch*

Propylon *'Before the entrance', a monumental gateway*

Proxenos *Representative of a foreign Greek city in Athens*

Prytaneis *The 50 'senators' of Athens, in permanent session*

Pylon *A gateway*

Rhymma *Cleanser used in bathing*

Skene *The permanent backdrop of a theatre*

Stlengis *A metal scraper used by bathers*

Stoa *A rectangular building fronted by a colonnade*

Strategoi *The ten elected generals of the Athenian army*

Symposion *An intellectual gathering, party and feast*

Theatron *The seating area of a theatre*

Tholos *A 'beehive tomb' from the Mycenaean period*

To neos *'The temple' – any temple, but also the Parthenon*

Trapezite *A 'table man', or moneychanger*

Trittyes *'Thirds' – a group of demes constituent of the phyllai*

USEFUL PHRASES

Excuse me *singignoske mi*

Hello *oule; chere*

Goodbye *chere; erroso*

Thank you *efcharistos im, charis si*

When? *pote?*

Where? *pou?*

Who? *tis?*

Why? *ti?*

Why not? *ti men?; ti gar?*

Yes *nai; nechi; malista; kai malista; tauta; tauta de*

No *Ou*

Can you tell me the way to [the Agora]? *Dineo an me ipin tin odon pros [tin agoran]?*

I want to buy wine, oil and fish. Where is the market? *Voulome oniste inon, eleon, ichthin. Pou estin i agora?*

How much is a bed for the night? *Tis estin i aksia pros kathevdin mia nikti?*

I have been robbed. Where is the magistrate? *Elizonto me. Pi estin o dikastis?*

I want to change my money into glaukai. *Voulome allatin ta emon chrimata is glafkas.*

I am ill. Where is the temple of Asklepios? *Asthenis imi. Pi estin o naos tou Asklipiou?*

I need to see my proxenos. *Di me idin ton emon proksenon.*

I want to buy a slave. When is the slave market? *Voulome oniste ena sklavo. Pi estin h agora sklavon?*

Is there a gymnasium nearby? *Estin en gumnasion plision?*

Where is the bathhouse? *Pi ta loutra isin?*

NOTES FOR THE MODERN READER

THE MODERN READER MAY WONDER WHAT BECAME OF ATHENS AND ATTICA IN THE TWO AND A HALF MILLENNIA AFTER THE PERIOD DESCRIBED IN THIS BOOK. THE FOLLOWING BRIEF HISTORICAL SURVEY COVERS THE END OF THE ATHENIAN EMPIRE, AND THE FALL OF GREECE TO A SUCCESSION OF FOREIGN INVADERS: THE MACEDONIANS, THE ROMANS, THE 'LATINS' AND, FINALLY, THE OTTOMAN TURKS. IN THE NINETEENTH CENTURY, GREECE FINALLY BECAME A SOVEREIGN STATE, WITH ATHENS AS ITS CAPITAL.

THE FALL OF ATHENS

In 404 BCE, the Spartans finally defeated the Athenians. For a brief period, the city was ruled by an oligarchy that was known as the 'Thirty Tyrants', but they were quickly expelled and the democracy restored.

In the next century, Athens recovered to a degree, but Greece, exhausted by over a century and a half of foreign and civil wars, fell prey to a new ruler, Alexander of Macedon (356–323 BCE), known to us as Alexander the Great. In the division of his empire that followed his death, his successors ruled the Greek city-states directly or as client states.

ROMAN AND BYZANTINE RULE

The Romans broke Macedonian power in the second century BCE, and officially incorporated Greece into their empire in 146 BCE. It was the Emperor Hadrian (76–138 CE) who considerably enlarged and embellished Athens, building a great many monuments, including a library, and finally completing the Olympeion (see p. 61), some 600 years after Peisistratos had been begun its construction.

In the fourth century CE, Athens, like the rest of the Roman world, became Christian, and under the reign of Theodosius the Great (347–395 CE), the traditional pagan cults were abolished and the temples closed or converted to Christian worship. The Parthenon and the Erechtheion, as well as the Temple of Hephaistos, all became churches.

Athens remained a part of the Byzantine (Eastern Roman) Empire until the thirteenth century, when Greece was taken over by crusaders from Western Europe.

GREEK CHRONOLOGY

2600–1600 BCE   **Minoan and Early Helladic:** Minoan culture based in Crete dominates the Mediterranean.

1600–1050 BCE   **Mycenaean period:** After the collapse of Minoan Crete, the Greek mainland is dominated by the Mycenaean city-states. The Greeks attack and take Troy.

1050–800 BCE   **Dark Ages:** Invasions by the Dorians and Aeolians bring about the fall of Mycenaean civilisation. Cities are destroyed, abandoned or drastically reduced in size.

800–480 BCE   **Archaic period:** The city-states of Greece re-emerge. New artistic forms emerge influenced by Egypt and the Near East. The war with Persia begins in 499 BCE.

480–323 BCE   **Classical period:** The Classical period begins with the destruction of Athens by the Persians, who are then defeated by the Allies led by Athens and Sparta. Athens grows in power and builds an empire, triggering a 27-year war with the Spartans. Athens is defeated in 404 BCE, but re-emerges in the following century.

323 BCE –146 CE   **Hellenistic period:** Greece becomes part of the Macedonian Empire of Alexander the Great. After Alexander's death, states are either part of the Macedonian successor states or independent clients.

146–330 CE   **Roman period:** The Romans break Macedonian power in the second century CE and incorporate Greece in their empire.

330–1204   **Byzantine period:** When the Roman Empire is divided into two, Greece becomes part of the Eastern Empire whose capital is Constantinople (Byzantium).

1204–1458   **Latin period:** When the Byzantine Empire is conquered by crusaders, Greece is split into several 'Latin' kingdoms.

1458–1832   **Ottoman period:** After the conquest of Constantinople, Greece becomes a province of the Ottoman Empire.

1832–1973   **Kingdom of Greece:** Greece becomes independent after a war of independence against her Ottoman rulers. The monarchy is eventually abolished in a military coup.

1974–present   **Republic of Greece**

LATIN TO OTTOMAN

From 1204 to 1458, Athens was ruled by a succession of 'Latin' rulers, meaning Roman Catholic Western Europeans, and not Greek Orthodox Christians from Constantinople. These included, in turn, the Burgundians, the Catalans and the Florentines.

In 1458, five years after the fall of Constantinople to the Ottoman Turks, Greece also became part of the Ottoman Empire. The temples that had once been churches became mosques, and their statues and friezes were defaced by Muslims who objected to representations of the human form.

Although it was damaged, the Parthenon was more or less intact until the Venetian siege of 1687, when a shell ignited powder stored in the building, causing substantial damage. This was compounded in the early nineteenth century by Lord Elgin (1766–1841), who removed many of the surviving metopes, frieze blocks and parts of the pediments, and shipped them to London, where they can still be seen in the British Museum.

INDEPENDENCE

Ottoman Athens effectively became a backwater of a much larger empire whose interests were always focused to the east and south.

As Ottoman rule faltered in the nineteenth century, champions of Greek independence, including Lord Byron (1788–1824), financed the Greek liberation struggle. In 1832, an independent Greek state was proclaimed with Athens as its capital. The city was finally handed over by the Turks to the new government of King Othon of Greece (1815–1867) in 1833.

Athens hosted the first modern Olympics in 1896, an honour that fell to the city once more in 2004.

BOOKS

Aeskhylos, *The Complete Plays of Aeschylus*, trans. by G. Murray.

Camp, J. M., *The Archeology of Athens* is one of the leading works on Athenian and Attic archeology. This illustrated guide, aimed at the serious student of Athenian archeology, contains very detailed descriptions of the buildings of the Acropolis and Agora.

Carawan, E. (ed.), *The Attic Orators* is a useful source of the collected speeches for jury trials by the Attic orators.

Casson, L., *Travel in the Ancient World* is the definitive study of travel in the ancient Greek and Roman periods.

Connolly, P. and Dodge, H., *The Ancient City* contains beautiful illustrations of the ancient cities of Athens and Rome and brings the classical city to life. The book also

includes detailed reconstructions of many public buildings and temples, as well as private houses.

Euripides, *The Complete Plays of Euripides*, Manchester: Manchester University Press.

Flacelière, R., *Daily Life in Greece at the Time of Pericles* is the classic text on daily life in the ancient Greek world by French scholar Robert Flacelière. He covers every aspect of life, with particular reference to the cities of Athens and Sparta, which had such contrasting political ideologies and social systems.

Garland, R., *Piraeus* is a history of the port city of Piraeus from prehistory to the modern period.

Hurwit, J., *The Acropolis in the Age of Pericles* is a scholarly yet approachable illustrated guide to the Periklean Acropolis, with pictures of the existing ruins as well as reconstructions of the main buildings.

Plato, *Complete Works*, edited by Cooper, J., and Hutchinson, D.

Roberts, J. W., *The City of Sokrates*, gives a very readable description of the city of Athens at the time of Sokrates, covering the main social and political institutions, daily life, the arts and historical events.

Simon, E., *The Festivals of Attica* is a study of the festivals of Athens and Attica during the Classical period; it boasts some extremely detailed descriptions of participants and events.

Sophokles, *The Complete Plays of Sophocles*, trans. by Claverhouse, R.

Villing, A., *Classical Athens*, is a glossy, illustrated guide to the classical city published by the British Museum.

WEBSITES

There is a wealth of information about ancient Greece available on the internet. While a search will yield many useful results, some of the best sites are:

www.ancientgreece.co.uk
The British Museum's stand-alone website for ancient Greece.

www.crystalinks.com/greece.html
Information on an impressive array of subjects in ancient Greece.

www.perseus.tufts.edu
The website of the classics department of Tufts University.

www.kronoskaf.com
Contains information about and impressive reconstructions of ancient Athens.

INDEX